Combating Discrimination
Persona Dolls in Action

Combating Discrimination
Persona Dolls in Action

Babette Brown

Trentham Books

Stoke on Trent, UK and Sterling, USA

Trentham Books Limited

Westview House	22883 Quicksilver Drive
734 London Road	Sterling
Oakhill	VA 20166-2012
Stoke on Trent	USA
Staffordshire	
England ST4 5NP	

First published 2001
Reprinted 2005

British Library Cataloguing-in-Publication Data
A catalogue record for this book is available from the British Library

1 85856 239 2

Designed and typeset by Trentham Print Design Ltd., Chester and printed in Great Britain by Cromwell Press Ltd., Wiltshire.

DEDICATION

To the Danish, Dutch and UK partners in the European project,
'Persona Dolls: education without prejudice'.

ACKNOWLEDGEMENTS

My special thanks to Sue Adler, Molly Arenstein, Ros Bayley, Cathy, David, Fiona and Jenny Brown, Marianne Egedal, Jan Ford, Brendah Gaine, Doreen Harris, Chris Henshaw, Tina Hyder, Kerryn Jones, Gillian Klein, Jane Lane, Maureen O' Hagan, Greta Sandler, Carol Smith and Anke van Keulan, for the books, ideas and emotional support they generously offered and especially for willingly and critically reading the manuscript.

Thanks also to Kogan Page Ltd for permission to use the extract 'Giant Steps' from *Tales for Trainers* by Margaret Parkin (1998), to Peter Brown for taking the photographs and to Conrad and Henrietta Lee and Natasha, Katie and Louise Brown for posing for them.

.

Contents

Foreword

An early years practitioner sits in front of her small group of children. On her lap is a large doll dressed as an ordinary boy – rather fat and wearing glasses. She introduces the doll to the children. 'This is Peter. He has a mum, dad, two sisters. They live on a housing estate. Peter is unhappy because the other children tease him and call him, 'Fatty four eyes'. ... At this point the practitioner asks the children what Peter feels, how they feel about Peter and how they could help Peter feel happier.

This is what Persona Dolls are all about. They are a magical conduit that enables children to understand feelings and examine the way they respond to children who are perceived as different and treated as different by their peer group. The children respond to the doll's stories and are able to express their feelings in a non-threatening environment.

This book introduces the reader to the concept of Persona Dolls which, thanks to Babette Brown, can now become an integral part of early years education in Britain. Through the Dolls, children are able to empathise and freely ask questions and discuss issues relating to the doll's characteristics, feelings, family and cultural background. Persona Dolls enable practitioners to introduce topics that may otherwise have been considered inappropriate or difficult for young children.

The Dolls come alive as you read their stories and the children's reactions to them. What a wonderful way to communicate complex concepts to very young children. I recommend Persona Dolls to all early years workers – incorporate them into your day to day work with children.

Maureen O'Hagan
Honorary Secretary UK National Executive Committee
World Organisation for Early Childhood Education
Organisation Mondial Pour L'Education Prescolaire (OMEP)

Introduction

Injustice anywhere is a threat to justice everywhere.
Martin Luther King in a letter from Birmingham jail,
Alabama 16/4/1963

Persona Dolls are different from other dolls because they are the practitioners' Dolls. They are used to try and prevent young children learning prejudiced attitudes and discriminatory behaviour while helping them unlearn any negative messages they might have already learnt. The Dolls are given personalities, family and cultural backgrounds, likes and dislikes and the stories that are created around them enable children to explore positive and negative emotions. In the process children deepen their identification and friendship with the Dolls – who become 'people' in the setting. If the Dolls are introduced at the beginning of the year they can progress through the same problems as the children have adjusting to the unfamiliar environment.

The aim is to develop children's ability to empathise with the Dolls and care about them, to recognise the ways in which they are the similar to and different from themselves and to learn that discriminatory behaviour hurts. Through their identification with the Dolls, children are helped to see the injustice of the situations being presented to them in the stories and are motivated to think of solutions. Being in the role of problem solvers and decision makers and having their ideas treated with respect helps boost their self-esteem and confidence. Having heard stories in which the Dolls are unfairly treated, they are more likely to act when someone is excluded from play or teased and put down. From the way they answer questions we can get an idea of how far they are developing non-discriminatory attitudes.

Although I had read about the Dolls, it wasn't until I became involved in a European Project, 'Persona Dolls: education without prejudice' with six project partners from Britain, Denmark and the Netherlands that I appreciated just how powerful they are. The Dolls and their stories provide an effective, stimulating and enjoyable way to raise equality issues with young children. We believe that children are likely to pick up prejudiced attitudes and discriminatory behaviour wherever they live. If their perceptions of people who are different from themselves are based on stereotypical thinking they will probably retain this misinformation, unless positive steps are taken to counter this learning. What they learn when they are young crucially influences their relationships, their academic progress, their future life.

This book suggests that knowing how to use Persona Dolls appropriately offers an effective way to build on children's sense of identity, self-esteem and confidence and to encourage them to respond to others with respect and sensitivity. But to do this effectively, practitioners as well as students need to reflect on their own attitudes and practices. The way we interact with children is at the heart of good educational practice. We help them become active, enthusiastic and independent learners by equally valuing all their cultures and communities and understanding how prejudiced attitudes and discriminatory practices influence their lives and the lives of others. Persona Dolls, with their individual personalities, life histories, likes and dislikes, provide us with a way forward.

As Nelson Mandela said at his inauguration as President of South Africa in 1994:

> No one is born hating another person because of the colour of his skin, or his background or his religion. People must learn to hate, and if they can learn to hate, they can be taught to love, for love comes more naturally to the human heart than its opposite.

The thinking behind this book has been especially influenced by the work of Paulo Freire, Louise Derman-Sparks, Glenda MacNaughton and Trisha Whitney.

Freire (1972) argues that all education has social and political consequences and that educators have a moral, social and political responsibility to be involved in education for social transformation. According to him, collaboration between practitioners and children develops through confronting real problems. He called this a 'problem-posing' approach and contrasted it with traditional education which he described as 'banking' – teachers make the deposits which the children receive, memorise and repeat. Educators, on the other hand, critically reflect on the social consequences of what they teach; they work against the existing inequalities and injustices children face in their daily lives and towards empowerment. The outcome gives the less powerful greater ability to control and participate in decisions about their lives. The emphasis in this book is on empowering children through Persona Doll storytelling sessions because the process involved encourages them to become critical explorers, decision-makers, problem solvers and activists. Persona Dolls provide practitioners with a powerful tool to challenge inequality and bring about change.

Louise Derman-Sparks (1989) has influenced the thinking and practice of early years practitioners, particularly in the USA, Australia, South Africa, Britain and other European countries – more than 200,000 copies of her book, *Anti-Bias Curriculum*, have been sold since its publication in 1989! She suggests that practitioners need to create the educational conditions that encourage all children to know about and appreciate their own identity and culture(s) without needing to feel superior to anyone else. The uniqueness of every child is emphasised, so that they realise that the differences between them are special. Through learning about each other and appreciating their diversity, children can recognise that teasing, harassing and abusing one another is unfair and hurtful. By using accurate and authentic materials and images and by including in the curriculum the diversity of family structures, languages, religions and learning styles, children are likely to interact comfortably within their home culture as well as in the dominant culture.

To achieve these objectives, Derman-Sparks proposes four anti-bias education goals. The first two enable children to feel good about who they are and comfortable with similarities and differences in others. The last two goals provide children with the tools they need to be able to resist bias and prejudice, to think critically and deepen their understanding of the concepts of fairness and unfairness. Crucially, children are encouraged to care about others and to act if they are discriminated against or if they witness discrimination.

Persona Dolls and their stories link with the four goals described by Derman-Sparks:

- they encourage children to empathise, feel good about themselves and about their own culture(s) while at the same time respecting other children and appreciating their cultures.

- children are helped to unlearn prejudiced attitudes and discriminatory behaviour, develop problem-solving skills and consider alternative strategies for action.

- by creating stories around Dolls with whom children have identified and from whom they can learn, it is possible to reduce ridicule and feelings of superiority while promoting self-respect and pride. If children and students have a strong sense of self-worth and a secure cultural identity they are more likely to resist bias directed at themselves and to want to stand up for others experiencing discrimination.

- the stories help to expose the misconceptions and prejudices children have learnt and help them unlearn them.

- providing children with opportunities to problem solve encourages them to think flexibly and critically. The children care about the Dolls and want to help them solve any problems they are facing.

The innovative writings of Glenda MacNaughton (1993, 1996, 1997, 1998 and 2000) have been incorporated into this book, particularly her research on the influence of Barbie dolls on identity development and on uncovering what four and five year old children think about equity and social diversity using Persona Dolls. The decision to include so much of her work reflects not only its quality but also the shortage of research on these issues.

Trisha Whitney (1999) taught me a great deal about Persona Dolls and how they can be used to combat discrimination and develop empathy and the concept of fairness. Her detailed and practical experience and real-life examples clearly illustrate the processes involved in introducing the Dolls and developing their stories.

Terms used in this book

Ableism is based on the concept of 'normality' as defined by people who are 'able bodied'. This way of thinking implies that people with disabilities are abnormal and of lesser value. Black people with disabilities are accorded even lower status than White people with disabilities.

I am using the commonly used terms **people with disabilities** and sometimes **disabled people**, although I support the claim made by many individuals and their organisations that it is not their impairments that are disabling them but prevailing attitudes and the way society is organised. For example, not being able to walk is an impairment, but lack of mobility is a disability which could be corrected by providing more lifts and ramps.

Black refers to people of African, Caribbean or Asian origin who experience racism and to those with Arab, Cypriot or Latin American backgrounds who may also experience prejudice and differential treatment because of their ethnicity. It also includes adults and children in mixed parentage families. This political definition was formulated to unite people of diverse origins and cultures in the fight against racism and at the same time to reflect the reality that various ethnic groups are affected even though they are not equally targeted. Acknowledging that all these groups experience racism entails recognising the vast differences in their cultural patterns and lifestyles and the fact that this definition is not acceptable to all those concerned – some do not see themselves as allies in a struggle against racism and others who do may not describe themselves as Black.

As with many other groups of people, there is disagreement about whether the term **Gypsy** or **Traveller** is the more acceptable. To try and avoid causing offence a number of people are using **Gypsy/Traveller** as a compromise. I am following their example.

Homophobia refers to the assumption that heterosexuality, i.e. the emotional and sexual relationship between men and women, is 'normal' and 'natural' and that homosexuality, i.e. the emotional and sexual relationships between people of the same sex, is 'abnormal' and 'unnatural'.

Lesbian refers to relationships between women, and **gay** to those between men but some people prefer the blanket terms homosexual or gay to cover both relationships.

Mixed parentage describes children and families in which one parent is Black and one is White, even though the term has racist overtones. An alternative term needs to be found but I do not have one to offer.

Parent(s) is used to refer to adults responsible for the caring and rearing of young children, for example, biological and adoptive parents, grandparents, foster parents and legal guardians.

Practitioners refers to all adults who work with and teach children, whatever their qualifications, for example, childminders, playgroup workers, nursery nurses, teachers, classroom assistants, lecturers and residential care workers.

'Race' is a political category and not a biological one. The belief that Black people are inferior to White people stems from Britain's colonial past and was used to justify the terrible treatment of slaves when Britain was the world's leading slave trader. Expanded and reinforced during the days of empire, the concept of 'race' is alive and well in Britain today, even though the 'scientific' theories which attempted to classify people according to their 'race' were repudiated more than 40 years ago. Few scientists today accept that there are biological grounds for distinguishing one group of people from another.

Racism refers to the deeply rooted but groundless belief that certain 'racial' groups are biologically inferior to others. It is expressed through individual attitudes and practices as well as through institutional policies and procedures – even when these are operated by fair-minded individuals. People are disadvantaged and discriminated against because of their skin colour, culture or ethnicity and as a consequence they have poorer job opportunities, health, housing and education. Addressing racism requires that we strive for equality of opportunity, access and treatment.

Although there are crucial differences between being an asylum seeker and a **refugee**, the term refugee is being used here to cover both groups. A refugee is someone who has fled a country and been given refugee status by the government of the new country. Refugee status protects a person from being returned to her/his own country. An asylum-seeker has fled from her/his home country and is seeking refugee status. By law, asylum-seekers must be placed in temporary accommodation while their asylum claims are processed.

Setting refers to all the statutory, voluntary and private early years services that cater for young children under eight.

Sexism refers to the belief that a person's sex determines her/his capabilities, behaviour and status. It impoverishes men and women, boys and girls by limiting horizons and restricting choices. There is a greater awareness of women's rights today but sexism continues to influence the quality of women's and girls' lives, their life chances and attitudes towards them.

The political term **White** refers to people in Britain whose skin colour indicates or European ancestry. Although they do not experience racism because of their skin colour some people of, for example, Irish or Jewish backgrounds have a long history of oppression and racial prejudice. However, being White, they have the option of merging whereas racism is ever-present in the lives of Black people.

Acts of parliament change names and they change procedures but they do not change people ... It is only people who create or allow change. Christian Schiller (1974)

I am in the world to change the world.
Kathe Kollwitz, German artist

1

Promoting empathy

The reasons why we need to develop children's capacity to empathise are discussed in this chapter. The findings of a research study highlight what we are trying to achieve when using Persona Dolls with children.

Persona Doll storytelling sessions empower children. They are also perfect vehicles for promoting active empathy. Through their identification and bonding with the Dolls and their involvement in the storytelling sessions, children can learn to empathise with the feelings of others, respect those who are different from themselves and adopt caring, supportive and sensitive attitudes towards them. According to Magne Raundalen, developing children's capacity to empathise should be our primary task. He argues that the people who are generally admired and looked up to have caring and empathetic personality characteristics in abundance, whereas these qualities are lacking in those who are despised and condemned for their inhumanity.

> When we meet a person lacking in aptitude to empathise with others' feelings and who even enjoys hurting other people, we call these people inhuman. Some of the most evil of people have got their names engraved into history, Eichmann, Bormann, Goebbels... [The names of] those who transform the pain of evil into energy to fight for justice and human rights shine in human history – Martin Luther King Jnr., Mother Theresa, Olaf Palme. (Raundalen 1991:7)

Studies have shown that White civil rights activists in the USA originated from homes characterised by strong humanitarian values, political activism and a radical, preaching climate of protest against injustice. It is interesting to note that many of those White people who became involved in the liberation struggle in South Africa also seem to have come from homes in which concern for others was fostered. There is no research to back this observation but the claim is reinforced (though unintentionally) by Hilda Bernstein in her book 'The Rift: the exile experiences of South Africans' (1994). A tiny minority of the people she interviewed were White South African activists and some of these volunteered information about their family background although they were not questioned about it. Most commented on the fact that their parents taught them to be respectful, courteous and caring towards people, to critically question everything and to stand up for right and justice. However, not all the activists had these childhood experiences. Some grew up in homes steeped in racism but were strongly influenced by the attitudes and views expressed by people outside the family:

For example:

> My father was chosen to go to the World Hitler Youth Festival in 1936 in Germany, and upon his return, he became a foremost leader of the Hitler Youth in South Africa ... We lived in Johannesburg...where all our neighbours were Jewish people. We went to the Johannesburg German school; and there, luckily for both my brother and myself, there were teachers who challenged the views that kids brought from their homes... And that changed my views – initially not on apartheid issues, but... that was the first step. (quoted in Bernstein 1994:259)

This example illustrates the fact that even though the influence of the home is generally paramount, we as practitioners have an important role to play in developing children's understanding, attitudes and behaviour. We are powerful people: through our actions and attitudes we can make a difference to the lives of the children and families we are working with, and to future generations. Persona Dolls and their stories provide an enjoyable and non-threatening way through which we can carry out this responsibility.

It seems reasonable to suggest that most parents want their children to grow up to be respectful, co-operative and compassionate. Children who have been encouraged to empathise are more likely to be considerate and caring of others, to respond actively to people in distress and to react when they encounter unfair and unjust situations. The pioneering study, *The Altruistic Personality: rescuers of Jews in Nazi Europe* (1988), conducted by Samuel P. Oliner and Pearl M. Oliner graphically illustrates how developing children's ability to empathise can affect their adult behaviour. I believe there are crucial and fundamental links between their findings and what we are trying to achieve when using Persona Dolls with children. The aim is not of course to encourage our children to become 'rescuers' but to highlight how building empathy, respect and a caring attitude when they are young can positively affect their outlook on life and their relationships and behaviour as adults.

When conducting their study on rescuers, the Oliners set out to answer the following questions:

- What led ordinary men and women to risk their lives on behalf of others when they knew that discovery would mean being killed on the spot or sent to concentration camps?

- What experiences, values, and personality characteristics impelled them to act while others stood silently by?

The hypothesis they offer is that:

> ... there may exist something called an 'altruistic' personality, that is, a relatively enduring predisposition to act selflessly on behalf of others, which develops early in life. For this reason we were interested not only in what our respondents did during the war and the circumstances of their war-time lives but also in their parents and their youthful characteristics and behaviours as well as their current behaviours. (Oliner and Oliner, 1988:3)

Having an altruistic personality does not imply that the person will always act altruistically, only that she/he is more likely than most people to make altruistic decisions. Similarly, the Oliners do not propose that early life experiences and personality inevitably determine an altruistic response but suggest, rather, that they are likely to influence perceived choices.

The Oliners traced and interviewed 406 non-Jewish people who had rescued Jewish adults and children, selecting them on three criteria: the rescuer had to be motivated by humanitarian considerations, had to have risked her or his life and to have received no remuneration of any kind. The activities of those chosen were corroborated by external documentation and their humanitarian motives confirmed by the rescued survivors themselves.

A sample of 126 non-rescuers was included, because the researchers needed to discover not only what the rescuers might have had in common but also whether these particular attributes were in some way different from other people's.

During the interviews rescuers and non-rescuers were asked questions about their upbringing and the atmosphere in their homes. It emerged that:

- rescuers' parents depended more on reasoning than physical punishment. The Oliners believed this to be important, because reasoning focuses children's attention on the consequences of their behaviour towards other people and their awareness of other's feelings, thoughts and well-being. It communicates a message of respect and trust that enables children to feel a sense of personal efficacy and warmth towards others.

- the tendency to be moved by pain distinguished rescuers from non-rescuers.

- rescuers were set apart from non-rescuers by their caring relationships and the values their parents had taught them which prompted and sustained their involvement. They became and remained involved by having seen and participated in direct humanitarian work organized by their parents.

- their commitment to actively protect or enhance the well-being of others did not emerge suddenly under the threat of Nazi brutality but was integrated into their lives long before the war began. It was a learned response that had become part of their character.

- as the parents of rescuers were less likely to stereotype Jews, they themselves tended to avoid blanket condemnations. Some took a principled stand – it was simply not right to treat people the way the Jews were being treated and they expressed anger and hate towards the Nazis who violated the principle of justice. In the words of two of the rescuers:

> I found it incomprehensible and inadmissible that for religious reasons or as a result of a religious choice, Jews would be persecuted. It's like saving somebody who is drowning. You don't ask them what God they pray to. You just go and save them.

> It was unfair that I was safe simply because I was born a Protestant. That was the main reason for me. What I did was a question of justice. It was a very humble thing because I was in a privileged situation compared with other people who didn't deserve their situation at all.

For most of the rescuers caring compelled action. Their compassion and responsibility for others led them to risk their lives – they could not be passive bystanders. During the interviews they recalled the values they absorbed from their parents and other influential people – responsibility, equality and respect.

For example:

> They taught me discipline, tolerance, and serving other people when they needed something. It was a general feeling. If somebody was ill or in need, my parents would always help. We were taught to help in whatever way we could Consideration and tolerance were very important in our family. My mother and father both stressed those feelings. My father would not judge people who lived or felt differently than he did. That point was always made to us.

> They taught me to respect all human beings.

> He taught me to love my neighbour – to consider him my equal whatever his nationality or religion.

> She taught me to be responsible, honest, to respect older people, to respect all people – not to tease or criticise people of other religions.

Motivated by empathy, these people felt the sufferings of the Jewish people so painfully that they had to act. An empathetic reaction aroused more than a third (37%) of rescuers to their first helping act. In both the following episodes the response was impulsive, an immediate reaction to the victim's condition. The impact of a face-to-face encounter with a distraught Jewish person proved overpowering for this Polish woman:

> In 1942, I was on my way home from town and was almost near home when M. came out of the bushes. I looked at him, in striped camp clothing, his head bare, shod in clogs. He might have been about thirty or thirty-two years old. And he begged me, his hands joined like for a prayer – that he had escaped from Majdanek and could I help him? He ... knelt down in front of me, and said, 'You are like the Virgin Mary.' It still makes me cry. 'If I get through and reach Warsaw, I will never forget you.' Well, how could one not have helped such a man? So I took him home, and fed him because he was hungry. ... He was shivering, poor soul, and I was shivering too, with emotion. (Oliner and Oliner 1988:189)

A Polish man responded in an entirely unexpected fashion when faced with a stranger he knew was in danger simply because she looked Jewish:

> In November 1942, I placed an ad in the paper because I was looking for a maid. The third woman I interviewed had a really Jewish appearance. I do not remember our conversation now, but I knew I could not let her out in the street because she would get caught immediately. I checked some references for her because I wanted to make sure she was not involved in any political activity – that was my main concern. I thought to myself, 'I am married, have a child, am in trouble myself. I live here unregistered, I trade illegally, I am a reserve officer. How can I let that woman go?' My conscience was telling me that she was sentenced to death because of her appearance. It was the only reason I helped; I couldn't let it happen. If somebody had told me before the interviews that I was going to take a Jewish woman as my maid, I would have said he was a madman. (Oliner and Oliner 1988:190)

Eighty seven per cent of rescuers were motivated by equity and care and this judgment was confirmed by 83% of rescued Jewish survivors. Survivors used essentially the same concepts of justice in describing their rescuers:

> They are very noble, very fine people. They felt that people should not be hurt for no reason at all. When they saw injustice, they felt they should do something... Whether it was religion or their sense of justice – they didn't mind paying the price for this.

Rescue allowed the rescuers to preserve their sense of integrity, personal responsibility and identity – their image of who they were. At the time they were interviewed, significantly more rescuers than non-rescuers were currently involved in community work:

> I did everything from the heart – I didn't think about getting something for it. My father taught me to be this way. I still feel this way now. I cannot refuse if somebody needs something. That's why I still help people – I'll do it until I don't have the strength to do it anymore. (Oliner and Oliner 1988:227).

After the war helpful non-rescuers tended to confine their activities to their families, their church or national communities and their own age groups whereas rescuers involved themselves in activities on behalf of other nationalities or religions, the disabled, the young, the aged and the sick.

> By their present words and deeds rescuers continue to reassure us that there are caring people in the world, people who have retained a basic faith in the value of committed human relationships and a sense of connectedness to humanity. In reflecting on the enduring significance of their wartime actions, they inform us that not all things can be measured in terms of external rewards alone, but that contributing to the quality of life for others is itself a most enduring reward. They acknowledge the reality of evil, of bad people and bad ideologies, but they also tell us that individual effort matters. They assure us that people can shape their own destinies rather than merely stand by as passive witnesses to fate or allow themselves to become nothing more than victimised objects. (Oliner and Oliner 1988:227).

Although the study emphasises the role of the home Oliner and Oliner argue that preparing children to be caring and socially responsible also involves practitioners. By ensuring that anti-discrimination permeates the curriculum and having practitioners committed to implementing it, we can imbue children with the humane attitudes towards other people that characterised the incredibly brave actions of the rescuers. Obviously, we fervently hope that they will never have to face a similar test but, as the authors of the Parekh Report of the Commission on the Future of Multi-Ethnic Britain (2000:6) observe, '*Every generation owes its successors a duty to bequeath them a better country than it inherited.*'

We shall overcome

By working with Persona Dolls within an anti-discriminatory context we can positively influence the lives of children and their families. But we need to recognise that struggling against injustice and oppression can be difficult, emotionally draining and isolating. Louise Derman-Sparks (1993:28) agrees:

> There are times when we feel discouraged, when we see all the obstacles but we need to get better at looking at our small victories, to be able to honour and celebrate them even though they are small and do not constitute the whole picture.

Apart from acknowledging and celebrating our successes, we can draw emotional support from people who are on the same wavelength as ourselves and build networks together with them. We have a responsibility and the power to work actively towards transforming society and to keep the vision alive – that one day all children will grow up free from racism, sexism and other oppressions.

Some quotes to inspire and motivate:

There are four kinds of people in the world:
People who watch things happen,
People to whom things happen,
People who don't know what is happening,
And people who make things happen.
Liz Willis and Jenny Daisley.

'First they came for the Jews
and I did not speak out –
because I was not a Jew.

Then they came for the communists
and I did not speak out –
because I was not a communist.

Then they came for the trade unionists
and I did not speak out –
because I was not a trade unionist.

Then they came for me –
and there was no-one left
to speak out for me.'
Pastor Niemoeller, victim of the Nazis.

Everybody has the capacity to change but some people die before they do.
Louise Derman-Sparks

Not everything that is faced can be changed, but nothing can be changed
until it is faced.
James Baldwin

If you're not part of the solution, you're part of the problem.
Elridge Cleaver in a speech in San Francisco 1935

And a story to end with:

This is a story about four people
named Everybody, Somebody, Anybody and Nobody.
There was an important job to be done and Everybody was asked to do
it.
Everybody was sure Somebody would do it.
Anybody could have done it, but Nobody did it.
Somebody got angry about that, because it was Everybody's job.

Everybody thought Anybody could do it
But Nobody realised that Everybody wouldn't do it.
It ended up that Everybody blamed Somebody
when Nobody did what Anyone could have done.
Source unknown.

2

Persona Dolls in action

This chapter highlights the issues that need to be taken into account when selecting Dolls, creating their personas and presenting them to the children.

Persona Dolls are being used, particularly in the USA, in a variety of ways. The number of Dolls and how often they are used depends on practitioners in each setting. Some people prefer to use them at a set time every day while others bring them out whenever they consider it appropriate. These Dolls are different from other dolls, as Kay Taus, the originator of the 'Persona Doll' concept explains:

> While Persona Dolls can look just like regular dramatic play dolls, they're different because they have individual identities just like the children in the classroom do. They have a family, they live in a certain town, in a particular house or apartment building, they have certain friends, and these things don't change. The individual identities for the dolls are created at the beginning of the year after the teacher knows all of the children in his/her classroom so that some of the dolls can reflect the physical characteristics, identities, lifestyles, and circumstances of the children in the classroom. (Taus 1987)

The Dolls are small friends who can have their own special place in the room – perhaps where they can 'see' what is going on and the children can see them. But because the Dolls 'visit' the children, it might be preferable to keep them in the practitioner's cupboard so the children see them only when they 'visit'. Some practitioners let children play with the Dolls, provided they ask permission and play appropriately with them. Taus believes that instituting a request process reinforces respect for the Dolls and their identities.

The Dolls and their stories can make an important contribution, particularly when they are integrated into an anti-bias curriculum and used by people who are respectful, sensitive and empathetic. They raise children's awareness and understanding of equality issues, extend their understanding of fairness, encourage them to want to support those who experience discrimination and gradually come to recognise that certain groups of people have less power and others have more. If children have a strong sense of self-worth and a secure cultural identity they are more likely to resist discrimination directed at themselves and also to want to stand up for others experiencing discrimination. The suggestions, strategies and procedures being offered here are not a recipe but a guide to inform, inspire and enable practitioners to:

- build on their understanding of anti-bias principles, reflect on their attitudes, evaluate practice and use their knowledge and skills to implement anti-bias practice confidently and empathetically

- arrange to have a series of in-depth discussions to raise issues, achieve consensus and commitment before introducing the Dolls into the setting

- examine their own values and attitudes as well as agreeing the philosophy and goals of the setting before introducing the Dolls

- plan long and short term goals and strategies before introducing the Dolls

- transfer their previous experience and skills with other dolls to the telling of Persona Doll stories

- when introducing a Doll, weave happy stories around it before telling stories that present emotional and social problems

- enjoy using the Dolls to uncover the misinformation and discriminatory messages children have picked up

- introduce creative activities that will be stimulating and fun to reinforce the messages the storytelling sessions were designed to spread.

The children know that these special Dolls are in fact 'dolls'. The Dolls become real to them because their lives and experiences reflect those of the children. Children get to know the Dolls personally, bond with them and respond thoughtfully and sympathetically to them. The physical and visual presence of the Dolls heightens their involvement with the stories and the issues that arise. The Dolls we select, how we present them and the stories we create can positively influence children's identity formation.

Constructing positive identities

The solid foundation on which a building needs to rest can be compared to a child's identity – that inner core which, from the beginning, must be carefully constructed and maintained. It involves a sense of belonging to a particular group and of knowing who one is. We influence this process because children often adopt and incorporate our gestures, behaviour patterns, attitudes and feelings, partly by imitation and partly as the result of having their actions praised or criticised. Through storytelling and creative activities we enable children to express themselves as individuals – to tell us or show us who they are. We bear a heavy responsibility.

We need to think carefully about the possible impact our choice of Dolls could have on children. Any doll can have a persona and stories woven around it but although some manufacturers are producing dolls that present positive images of and for all children there are not enough of them. Chapter 10 offers information about some of the suppliers whose products counter discrimination and promote respect for a range of lifestyles and cultures.

Although Barbie is one of the most popular dolls on the market, the work of MacNaughton (1997) suggests that dolls like Barbie should not be used as Persona Dolls. She points out that although it is generally agreed that she influences young children's identity formation, there is controversy about whether Barbie and her various accessories in fact extend identity options, particularly of girls. Those who believe that the consequences are positive include, not surprisingly, Mattel – the company that produce her. They claim that presenting Barbie doing a range of non-traditional jobs raises children's awareness of occupations open to girls and extends their aspirations. For example, in 1965 Barbie was the first female astronaut in the USA to go into space and she has since been portrayed in many non-traditional occupations, such as surgeon, UNICEF ambassador and air force squadron leader. Barbie, they argue, is a positive role model for whom the sky's the limit!

Bob Dixon (1987) and Glenda MacNaughton (1997) both strongly oppose this view because they believe that Barbie:

- presents children with strong sex-role stereotypes that reinforce ultra-feminine ways of being

- presents children with a very upper class view of life. For instance, we never see Barbie dressed for the factory floor. She is only ever dressed for high-paid middle-class jobs. She always lives in large, well-appointed houses and her cars and clothes are of the luxury variety

- presents a world in which girls are rewarded for being pre-occupied with their appearance. You get your man or your job if you know how to look glamorous, groom your hair well, etc.

- presents boys and girls with the image of woman as sex-object

MacNaughton explored how children make sense of the identity options offered by Barbie. One-to-one interviews were conducted with 4-to-5 year olds in which they were asked what they knew and thought about Barbie and Barbie related products. They were also observed during two-hour free play sessions in which a large bag of Barbies and her products were placed in the centre of the block play area. Their play was recorded on video and MacNaughton used five of these transcriptions to discuss the identity implications it revealed. Most of the ten girls and eleven boys involved in these five sessions were from a Vietnamese-speaking background. MacNaughton describes the process by which the girls and the boys took, used, applied and absorbed or discarded Barbie as 'consuming' Barbie.

Overall, the girls rarely used Barbie for dramatic play with clear story lines. The short bursts of dramatic play that did occur were usually based on the story lines suggested by Barbie's packaging.

For instance, Ballerina Barbie was used to let Barbie twirl on the bars provided, and their play with Shopping Barbie involved loading up the trolley and going shopping. The girls regularly talked with each other as they played. They generally shared information about the Barbie they were playing with or about their own Barbies and her products.

MacNaughton suggests two inter-related features of the girls' play:

- Their constant grooming and dressing of her indicated that they were consuming Barbie as a generalised female identity, concerned with appearance and her accessories.

- Their insistence on matching specific clothing and accessories with specific Barbies as presented and packaged by Mattel indicated that they were consuming Barbie as specific female identities who could teach, shop, dance and perform athletic feats.

Barbie's physical design linked the girls into a dependent relationship with Mattel's packaging messages, They interpreted their failure to make Barbie 'work' as she was supposed to as being a consequence of not following the instructions carefully enough or having misunderstood them. They learnt to look to Mattel's packaging to tell them 'how to construct their imaginative world' and to mistrust what they themselves did with Barbie. They were also learning about friendship. When dressing and grooming Barbie, other girls will be your friends but boys will often disrupt, hassle, take your Barbies and invade your space.

As far as the boys were concerned, it was the physical appearance of Barbie's body rather than her clothes that was paramount in determining their play. Their constant undressing of Barbie indicated that they were consuming her as a doll whose specific identity could be stripped through making her naked. Once naked, Barbie was created in a variety of ways – as a doll, a gun or an object to hit others with. The boys needed to do this in order to play with her. The key aspect of her body that resounded in their consumption of Barbie was her breasts or, as several of the boys called them, 'her boobies'. Mattel has constantly denied that Barbie's breasts are sexualised but for the boys in this study they clearly were. Perhaps this should come as no surprise given that Barbie was modelled on a doll made for adult males in post-war Germany! The girls saw that boys preferred Barbie nude and that her nudity was seen as funny and at times naughty. The boys were consuming an identity option that defined women and girls through their body as an object, particularly a sex object to be held, laughed at and giggled over. While consuming Barbie their relationship with each other and the girls meant that they were consuming an identity option which defines harassing the girls and sexual innuendo as a source of friendship and pleasure for boys.

Although this was a small study, I think it is reasonable to support MacNaughton's claim that play with Barbie restricts rather than expands children's exploration of gender identity options. Consequently, I believe that dolls like Barbie should not be used for telling Persona Doll stories because they limit children's opportunity to explore a wide range of identity options.

Selecting appropriate Dolls

We need to think about which equality issues affect the lives of the children in our group so that we choose Dolls which will provide us with opportunities to talk about the diversity in our setting. We will probably start with only one or two Dolls and steadily build up the collection so we can introduce diversity outside the children's immediate experience. We should ensure that the collection consists of a good mix of boy and girl Dolls because it is possible that some children may never have come across boy dolls before and may think that dolls have to be female. Through the personas we create we challenge gender stereotypes by, for example, including in a boy Doll's persona that he enjoys playing in the home corner or that his favourite colour is pink. Being familiar with each Doll's persona enables us to choose those that most closely fit the situations and the feelings portrayed in the stories.

Selecting Dolls should be a team effort. The Dolls we choose need to be appealing not only to the children but to us too. We also need to think of and treat the Dolls as friends – 'people' we are interested in and care about. Whether we are buying or making the Dolls, we should ensure that we include not only various shades of skin colour but also a range of hair textures, facial features and body shapes. It's also important to think about which groups children may be learning stereotypes about and to ensure that the Dolls we choose reflect these groups as accurately as possible. Particular care needs to be taken that the Dolls we buy or make do not reinforce a golliwog image – wide grinning mouth, prominent round eyes and 'woolly' hair. Many Black adults recall their pain and humiliation when, as children, they were taunted and compared to golliwogs.

Our collection of realistic, loveable Dolls should have the skin tones, eye shapes, hair textures, gender, languages spoken, religion, socio-economic class, family makeup, physical abilities, ethnic and cultural backgrounds that are similar to the children in the setting. Children need to be able to relate to particular features that they share with the Dolls, for example, 'She's got braids just like me'. But we also need Dolls with physical characteristics and identities that reflect families and communities that are not represented in the setting. For example, if there are no children with disabilities in the group, the children will nevertheless be able to become friends and empathise with the Dolls who have a variety of disabilities. Used in a setting in which a range of lifestyles, traditions and cultures are valued, carefully chosen Persona Dolls and their stories encourage children to appreciate diversity.

To ensure that stereotypical images are not being created we need to uncover our own stereotypical thinking and check that any such notions are not unconsciously being reinforced. If possible, parents should be involved in the making and the buying, to ensure that the Dolls and the clothes are physically and culturally appropriate and that disabilities are accurately portrayed. By involving parents at the outset and sharing with them the reasons for using the Dolls they are enabled to 'own' them.

Buying the dolls

As caring adults we need to check carefully that the facial features of the dolls we choose – eyes, nose, lips and cheekbones – accurately portray the children being represented. Avoid dolls that are white figures painted brown/black – their features will not be accurate. If the dolls have hair, the texture needs to be authentic. Ideally, they should have different hairstyles. Try to ensure that the 'skins' of the dolls are of different shades and if the dolls are dressed, check that brown and black dolls do not have white bodies underneath – there are unfortunately dolls like these on sale in shops and available from early years equipment catalogues! It is a good idea to select anatomically correct Dolls, as they will help young children to appreciate that being a girl or a boy depends upon their anatomy – many children are uncertain!

Persona Dolls reflecting a variety of impairments can heighten children's awareness and understanding and help them begin to appreciate similarities and differences and to recognise that there are different degrees of impairment. For instance, that some people who are visually impaired see with the aid of glasses whereas those who are blind might use white sticks or have guide dogs. Children can also be helped to understand the frustrations and problems adults and children with physical impairments have to cope with, for example, when they go shopping, visit friends and want/need to go into public buildings like cinemas and offices.

Dolls representing, for example, Down's Syndrome can be bought, as well as aids such as crutches, wheelchairs, hearing aids and glasses for smaller Dolls. Parents should be consulted before the dolls are bought, as not everyone is happy with them. Some suppliers are listed in chapter 10.

Making the Dolls

We may have to make the Dolls or arrange to have them made, because those that accurately represent a range of skin colours and physical features are not generally available. In any case many people prefer to have cloth Persona Dolls because they are likely to be unique and special – different from the dolls in the home corner. Another advantage is that they are more huggable. Parents can be asked to help make the dolls and their clothes, especially if there is a child in the group with, let us say, a particular disability and the appropriate doll is not commercially manufactured. Parent involvement ensures that the dolls and their clothes will be culturally appropriate and that physical features are accurately portrayed.

It is a good idea to keep the body pattern simple. The stuffing should be loose enough to ensure that the Dolls can sit and bend their arms but their necks should be firm so that they can hold their heads up – unless a particular Doll is representing a child with little muscle control. When selecting the stuffing keep health and safety in mind.

The Dolls can be any height but 20-30 inches is a good size for children to identify with and clothes are easy to get hold of. Like the children in the setting, the Dolls should be thin, fat, short and tall.

Dolls, like the children, have different skin tones. To get the appropriate ones coloured fabrics from light beige to ebony brown are needed. Hair too must be appropriate and be able to stand up to a certain amount of handling. The most effective way is to adapt adult wigs but this requires skill and can be expensive. Using hot glue is the fastest way to stick strands of hair – it is clear and dries quickly. Wool can be attached across the top of the head and left to hang loosely down to the Doll's shoulders; it can be plaited and then sewn or glued. Beads can be added. It may be possible to buy curly hair in a couple of colours from craft shops. A thick head of hair can be produced by putting the individual strands as close together as possible. To portray very short hair use thick acrylic paint, spread it on thickly and represent strands of hair by making ridges.

Individual ethnically appropriate faces can be embroidered or created with thick acrylic paint, using a few lines and a bit of shading. Use a small brush and start with the eyebrows and eyes and work down the face, letting the paint dry between colours. Keep the faces simple and unique – they don't have to be perfect faces! An important tip: make sure the glue and paint have dried properly before dressing the Dolls.

Clothes can be made or bought from street markets, charity shops or donated by parents – tiny jeans, teeshirts, sweat-shirts, dresses and coats are made for little babies these days and will fit larger Dolls. Choose clothes and accessories that reflect the personal qualities of the Dolls and the children in the setting. Have a supply of extra clothes so that the Dolls don't always wear the same ones when they visit!

Children's cheap sunglasses with the lenses taken out can be used for large Dolls who are visually impaired. These can be bought at street markets but usually only in summer. The Ear, Nose and Throat department of hospitals, health clinics, and GPs may be able to provide hearing and other aids.

Getting to know you, getting to know all about you

Once the Dolls have been selected or made, the next step is to create a detailed persona for each one. It is a decision making process in which all practitioners and, if possible, parents draw on their knowledge, understanding and commitment to equality as well as on their imagination. To ensure that the Dolls reflect the children in the group everyone has to agree details such as gender, ethnicity, class, family structure, type of home, religion, cultural background, languages spoken, physical features, skin colour, special abilities and disabilities, likes and dislikes. Every time a new Doll is added to the collection everyone needs to discuss and agree its persona. If a setting plans on introducing a Doll to reflect a child with a particular impairment it may be a good idea to consult not only with parents but also with the organisation concerned. Supportive organisations are listed in chapter 10.

The Dolls will have a great deal in common but each will be unique. Their basic details remain constant. When new children join the group only small changes in family structures or personal details will probably need to be made to ensure that the Dolls reflect the new lot of children. If the intake has changed, however, the personas of some of the Dolls may no longer reflect the children. Accordingly, when the children who know the Dolls leave the setting, the Dolls can be given new personas before being introduced to the new arrivals.

Once the Dolls' personas have been created, it is advisable to check that the family history, culture, language and religion are accurate and hang together, and that there is sufficient information about each Doll including:

its name and age

the language(s) it speaks

its family and cultural background

its social class

its family structure, for example, two parents, single parent, gay or lesbian

its family members – including adopted, fostered and step-children and step-parents

the length of time the family has been in this county (if relevant)

its refugee experiences (if any)

where it lives

its diet and food preferences and how food is eaten

routines such as getting up in the morning and going to bed

days of special significance and how they are spent

its favourite activities, books, songs and TV programmes

Things it is able and unable to do.

Once their personas are established, give the Dolls names that fit their personalities and particular family and cultural backgrounds. Keep a record of each persona and of the details added during the storytelling sessions. Jones and Mules (1997:13) suggest that:

> Consistency and continuity are very important elements in the development of a doll's persona and the stories attached to it. Keeping a **diary** of each doll's life can help to maintain consistency and ensure continuity. The diary can contain a description of the doll's persona, the stories that are told to the children about the doll... Practitioners can date and record which children are present for each story, some of their responses to the stories and any issues that were raised... Diary records will also allow other or new practitioners to continue using the doll... Some people like to **tape record** the sessions where persona dolls are used to keep a record of the children's responses to the stories and the issues raised. These tapes can also be used to pick

up on unresolved issues or other issues raised by the children in response to the story.

Becoming friends

According to Whitney (1999:26), we should spend time getting to know each Doll, especially before introducing it to the children for the first time. By taking it home with us for a couple of days it can become more 'alive', and this will make it easier for us to present it to the children and for them to accept it as 'real'.

It might be an idea to start with a boy Doll to captivate the boys, especially those who feel they have to project a macho image. At first, present only one Doll at a time to the children. The goal is simply to introduce it and establish and develop the children's relationship with it. The Doll won't need to have a story to tell because the time will be taken up giving three or four details about its likes and dislikes, habits, special interests. Involve the children by asking questions on the Doll's behalf, for example: Robert wants to know what foods do you like best? Children may express very negative feelings towards unfamiliar foods and we will need to intervene. Remember that when we stimulate children to ask questions we need to be prepared as far as possible to answer the ones they might ask!

If the setting has a range of Dolls ensure that all are used so that the diversity of their personalities and situations is represented and enjoyed. When a story mirrors a specific characteristic of a child in the setting, the Doll chosen should have a similar characteristic but needs different ones also. Provide a special chair for the Doll to sit on when its story has been told so it can be cuddled and talked to, especially by the children who have experienced the particular situations or feelings described in the story. Children who have had a strong emotional reaction to a story or on whom a particularly difficult story was mirrored are likely to welcome the opportunity to spend some quiet time with the Doll – they may use it as a special friend and confidante.

There is one no right way to use Persona Dolls. A great deal depends on the personality and experience of the person telling the story. All the practitioners need to know about the persona each Doll has been given so that the children receive consistent information when they ask questions. But although the aim is to build the confidence and storytelling skills of everyone, some people may not feel comfortable enough about doing so. The problem is that somebody who is particularly good at telling Persona Doll stories may unintentionally deter others and, in time, consider this her/his domain, as happened in one Australian childcare centre, as described in a letter written to me by a friend.

> Although a few of us were part of the initial discussions and planning only one person really used the dolls – she was brilliant! I think the reason she told persona doll stories to all the children in the centre was because she was already comfortable as a storyteller. Once she got started though, I think she became quite possessive of the dolls. It was her niche at the centre, and as an unqualified child care worker I think she felt empowered by that. I don't think anyone wanted to challenge the position that she had created so no one else picked up on the dolls although I think they agreed that the concept and the critical thinking and problem-solving aspects had great potential.

Knowing how to use Persona Dolls appropriately offers an effective way to build on children's sense of identity and self-esteem. Children are helped to deal with situations where they have been discriminated against or they see others being treated unfairly. They develop the confidence and skills they need to act in these situations.

Even children who have limited understanding or the vocabulary to express their ideas and experiences can empathise with the Dolls. They can be encouraged to touch and gently explore physical, colour and textual differences. One of the Dutch partners on the European 'Persona Doll Project: Education Without Prejudice' works with children up to the age of two years. She encourages them to empathise with a Doll called Kyril. On one occasion she told them a short story about Kyril having a cold. The children were each given a small piece of tissue and as he was carefully passed around the group, they tenderly wiped Kyril's nose. She believes that a short beginning and ending ritual every time the Doll visits helps to make the children feel secure – they know what is going to happen next. She reports that, '*When I ask the children, 'Shall we sing Kyril's song?' they are beside themselves with enthusiasm and immediately point to the place where he is kept'.*

Participants on a training course in Sheffield concluded that Persona Dolls could be used with children under three. The participants, who included Sure Start Outreach and Playworkers, felt that the Dolls could play an important role in group settings and with parents in their homes. They suggested introducing a mix of happy, everyday issues to build confidence and self-esteem as well as 'heavier' issues surrounding, for example, racism, bullying and discrimination. It was felt that matters such as bereavement and parents separating could be more effectively dealt with on a one-to-one basis. These are a few of the issues identified that very young children are likely to be interested in and respond to:

- the Doll has a sore finger – encouraging empathy and identification

- comfort blankets – Doll has lost blanket – encouraging empathy

- it moves house

- it's excluded from playing by big sister/brother because it is too small – introduces fairness and unfairness

- Doll stays at Dad's/Mum's house – is lucky to have two bedrooms/two homes

- going to the doctor/dentist/hospital/optician

- differences – skin colour, hair texture. Using two or three Dolls can encourage the children to notice differences and talk about them.

Dolls and their personas

This is Thandanani. She is nearly 5 years old. She was born in London and so were her parents and her baby brother William. Her grandma was born in Trinidad and her nan in Scotland. Grandma lives with them and looks after her and William when mum and dad go to work. Mum's a teacher and dad's a librarian. Grandma is teaching Thandanani to speak Creole. Her favourite food is rice and peas but she also loves sausages and chips. She doesn't like tomatoes,

Thandanani.

plantains or chicken. Her favourite toys are her teeny-tiny teddy, her bicycle, her dolls and lego. She's very good at running and hopping but she can't catch a ball. She wants people to call her Thandanani and not Narni and to leave her hair alone!

This is Heather. She is 6 years old. She lives on the ground floor of a block of flats with her mum and her two big sisters, Rebecca and Penny. In the holidays they go to their dad's farm but mum doesn't go with them – that makes Heather a bit sad. But she has great fun when she is on the farm. She's learning to ride a small pony. There is something Heather doesn't like and that's school. She does like her teacher but not the children. They laugh at her because they say she's

25

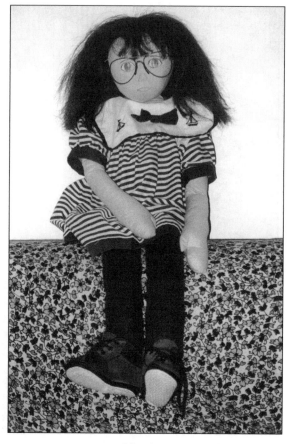

Heather

silly and stupid. Sometimes they play with her but sometimes they don't. Her favourite food is pasta and pizza and she loves playing with her dolls and her beanies. She wishes she didn't have to wear glasses.

This is Bobby. He is 3 years old. He lives with his two mothers, Sara and Liz, in a flat next door to a park. Every Sunday he goes to Sunday School while they're in church. They both work in a factory and Charlie goes to a childminder. He enjoys painting and making things and is learning to cut with scissors. He wishes he had somebody to play with – there are no big children like him at his childminder, only babies. But when he goes home he's very happy

Bobby

because his best friend Kushtrim who lives next door comes to play. They both love puzzles, drawing, watching TV and listening to stories.

Persona Dolls can encourage children to:

- enjoy stories and become actively engaged

- introduce children to social diversity with which they have little or no experience or knowledge

- enable all children to gain an awareness and understanding of the richness and diversity of different lifestyles

27

- encourage children to value each other equally

- provide opportunities for children to see their own individuality and life experiences valued within the daily programme

- help children learn about dealing with unfairness against themselves and others

- develop anti-discriminatory attitudes and strategies so they can confidently stand up for themselves and for others. Unlearn prejudices, misconceptions and stereotypes

- think critically and reject discriminatory actions, attitudes and ideas

- broaden their vocabularies by learning and using words that describe how the Doll(s) are feeling and words that express their own emotions

- feel supported – realising that others have the same or similar experiences. Simply hearing that there are possible solutions can be supportive

- build strong and positive identities so they feel good about themselves

- feel secure enough to express their feelings and experiences, be able and willing to admit mistakes and to transfer the skills they have learnt to experiences and situations they meet in their lives

- recognise and empathise with the feelings of the Doll(s)

- be compassionate, respectful and caring of others, be willing and able to listen to and learn from them, respond with respect and sensitivity and appreciate how their own behaviour affects other people

- learn group problem-solving skills, be able to think critically and evaluate a number of solutions and choose the ones most likely to succeed

- explore and compare the similarities and differences they encounter

- resist the negative impact of racism and other oppressions on their development so that as adults they will want and be able to work towards bringing about change.

Persona Dolls encourage us to:

- help children feel comfortable interacting with others

- develop our own active listening skills and ability to acknowledge and accept each child's responses and give positive feedback

- use the Dolls pro-actively i.e. before a problem presents itself

- present clear and correct information in an attention-getting way

- be able to raise challenging issues with children that they might previously have been reluctant to talk about

- become more aware of our own stereotypes of people, to develop our anti-discriminatory attitudes and be able to actively challenge discrimination

- challenge the belief that White, non-disabled adults and children, (especially if they also have long blonde hair and blue eyes) are perceived as being most beautiful and desirable

- help children to deal with their anxieties and fears

- avoid imposing our ideas on children – be able to step back and let the children identify the Doll's feelings, think critically and problem solve

- turn the culture of the group towards caring, respect and support and away from teasing, name-calling and exclusion.

Using Dolls while telling stories makes it easier for children to make connections with their own lives. They are empowered to reflect on who they are and on the identities and feelings of those around them. Using Persona Dolls to raise issues broadens all children's intellectual horizons. It develops their ability to empathise with and relate to others. Working with Persona Dolls can also positively influence our own attitudes and practice.

---

* Dolls available from: Persona Doll Training, 51 Granville Road, London N12 05H.

3

Persona Dolls are powerful!

This chapter spells out some of the ways in which Persona Dolls can help to combat biased attitudes and discriminatory behaviour. Research findings suggest how the Dolls can be used to uncover the prejudices and misinformation that children may have picked up from the world around them.

There is nothing new about using dolls and puppets when telling children stories. People have been doing it for years, sometimes just for fun but also, more seriously, to raise children's awareness. Puppets are being used to alert children to the dangers of taking drugs, drinking and Aids. Ros Bayley (1995), for example, uses them to raise health education issues with young children.

Persona Dolls can be used to explore a wide range of topics but the focus of this book is on countering the values, stereotypes and prejudices that underpin racism and other social inequalities and on supporting those who experience discriminatory and unequal treatment. I hope that readers will be inspired and empowered to draw on their previous experience with dolls or puppets to start exploring this exciting and innovative approach.

An initial reaction may be that young children are being introduced to ideas and experiences that will be of little interest to them. However, Tizard and Hughes (1984:128) showed that by the age of 4 children's curiosity about and concern for other people is well established:

Interest in other people – both children and adults – was a characteristic feature of most of the children in the study and manifested itself in many different topics: their friends, other members of the family, growing up, birth, illness and death, what people did for their living and so on. Indeed, it is worth remarking on the breadth of the children's interests, and the complexity of the issues which they raised. It is sometimes supposed that children of this age have special childish interests mainly to do with mothers, babies, dolls, teddies and animals ...The conversations in our study suggest that, on the contrary, all human experience was grist to their intellectual mill.

Issues are raised through stories based on the day to day experiences that capture children's interest and promote participation. When developing the Dolls' personas, creating scenarios and facilitating group discussion we need to take account of the pivotal role that gender plays in children's lives.

Gender needs to be understood as a way of being, thinking, experiencing and feeling that drives and influences development. Children's gender influences every aspect of their development, from their values, beliefs, language, emotion, imagination, cognition and style of communication to their involvement in physical activities, use of space and social relationships... It is also important to be aware of what specific aspects of the gender factor in children's development need to be challenged and/or supported through an anti-bias curriculum. (MacNaughton 1996:54)

To be able to create personas and stories that reflect the children and the situations they experience, we need to observe children carefully. In the process we pick up on their power relationships and by incorporating this knowledge into stories we offer support to children who need it and at the same time attempt to change discriminatory attitudes. Children's identification with Persona Dolls is often profound and arouses strong emotions. Their behaviour, attitudes, relationships with the other children in the group and the way they see themselves can be affected. Working with such a powerful tool we need to be particularly sensitive and principled, treating each child with equal concern, selecting culturally and physically appropriate Dolls and creating stories that convey positive messages.

Through discussions with other practitioners, we can develop effective ways to present issues to children that are emotional or complicated.

By providing plenty of opportunities to share and identify with the feelings and situations the Dolls experience, we develop young children's ability to empathise. Raundalen (1991) believes that their capacity to empathise should be encouraged and nurtured as much as possible, although there is controversy over whether young children are, in fact, capable of empathising. Piaget (1977) argues that children are egocentric so cannot see the world from other people's points of view i.e. cannot decentre. Margaret Donaldson (1978) on the other hand showed that the ability to decentre is dependent not on children's developmental stage, as Piaget claimed, but on how tasks are presented to them. She proposes that young children do less well on the tasks on which Piaget based his theory because these tasks were unrelated to their own knowledge and experience. Their performance on tasks that related to what they already knew and that were embedded in an appropriate context was far better than on Piaget's unrelated tasks. Dunn (1993:109) also believes that young children are capable of decentring, arguing that even toddlers recognise and respond to other people's feelings and improve or worsen their emotional state in practical ways. Young children can be supportive, concerned, intimate and humorous or they can be manipulative, devious and teasing and deliberately upset other people.

The study by Oliner and Oliner (1988) described in chapter one highlights the importance of developing children's capacity to empathise. The non-Jews who rescued Jews had acquired from their parents a strong sense of responsibility and a caring attitude towards others in distress – they felt their pain and acted to alleviate it.

> It [empathy] begins in close family relationships in which parents model caring behaviour and communicate caring values. Parental discipline ... includes a heavy dose of reasoning ... Simultaneously, however, parents set high standards they expect their children to meet, particularly with regard to caring for others. They implicitly or explicitly communicate the obligation to help others in a spirit of generosity, without concern for external rewards or reciprocity. Parents themselves model such

behaviours, notably in relation to their children but also toward other family members and neighbours. Because they are expected to care for and about others while simultaneously being cared for, children are encouraged to develop qualities associated with caring. Dependability, responsibility, and self-reliance are valued because they facilitate taking care of oneself as well as others. (Oliner and Oliner 1988:249-50).

Children are more likely to be able to empathise if they feel good about themselves. Jenny Mosely (1993) proposes that self-esteem is the inner picture we all have of ourselves. It is the value we give to our strengths and our weaknesses.

She believes that:

- we have low self-esteem if we think we are useless, incompetent, unpopular and of little use to society

- if we have sound self-esteem, we know we are capable, competent, liked and valued and we believe we can lead useful lives in society

- self-esteem is shaped from an early age by the important adults in a child's life. Too much criticism, too many don'ts, too few cuddles, too little praise and encouragement when we are young leads to low self-esteem and feelings of failure

- a child who feels a failure may have trouble making friends, fitting in, or doing their best

- a child who has sound self-esteem has a better chance of being successful in all areas of school life and of being confident to learn new things

- it is helpful for all children if the important adults in their life work together to share the same values and expectations

- parents and teachers working together towards the same goals can do much to build children's self-esteem and make their lives happier and more fulfilled.

Equality matters

Children need to feel that they belong in the group – this boosts their confidence and builds their identity.

Children notice similarities and differences – we encourage them to do so through, for example, drawing their attention to things that are the same and those that are different. They begin to realise the ways in which they and their family are the same and different from other children and their families, develop a sense of their own identity and in the process decide which groups they belong to and which they don't. They start making judgements about adults and children different from themselves – some they perceive positively, i.e. as being good, and some as negative i.e. as being bad. They learn that some differences are valued and some are not and that it is OK to treat certain groups of people unequally. These judgements are influenced by prevailing attitudes expressed, for example, by adults, other children, TV, and books. If their perceptions of people different from themselves are based on stereotypical thinking it is likely that they will retain this misinformation for the rest of their lives unless active steps are taken to counter this learning. Excerpts from interviews with Hawai'in children who had just been shown a video clip from the film, *Swiss Family Robinson* illustrate this process:

This is how four 5-6 year olds responded:

Interviewer	Were there good guys and bad guys?
Kenchiro	Yeah!
Interviewer	Who were the good guys and who were the bad guys?
Keoni	The good guys were in the house.
Kenchiro	The guys with the beard. Those was bad guys and the good guys were on the mountain.
Interviewer	Who were the bad guys?
Dylan	The ones who was attacking.
Elijah	The ones with swords and stuff.
Interviewer	In that short amount of time, how can you tell who is a bad guy and who is a good guy?
Keon	'Cause the good guys don't have, uh, hats.
Elijah	Or weapons.

Kenchiro: Cause the good guys are smarter than the bad guys. Tobin (2000:125)

The reactions of 7-8 year olds:

Interviewer Who were the good guys in that movie?

Nolan The ones that was winning.

Mary-Jean The one with the coconut bombs.

Interviewer Were there any bad guys in the movie?

Derek Yeah. The Indians.

Interviewer How could you tell they were bad?

Nolan Because they tried to kill them.

Derek Yeah. They were trying to attack.

Interviewer Is there a difference between the way the good guys and the bad guys look?

Mary-Jean No.

Derek Yeah. Because one was the Indians and one was the Americans.

Interviewer Which were the good ones?

Nolan The Americans.

Interviewer Which were the bad ones?

Derek The Indians.

Interviewer Anything else on how they looked?

Nolan Yeah. The Indians has knives and stuff?

Interviewer Is that how Indians are?

Nolan Yeah.

Derek And good guys have tricks and bombs. Tobin (2000:80-81)

The question arises as to how Indians got into the conversation at all, since the location of the film is a tropical island and the 'bad' guys are played by Asian and Polynesian actors dressed as pirates. Children in Hawaii, where Tobin conducted the study, know very little about Indians from India but they know a good deal about American 'Indians'.

> What I find disturbing about Derek's and Nolan's mistakes is that I fear it is what they know and think about Native Americans that leads them to call the bad guys in the movie Indians. What makes me cringe is that these children are using the word *Indian* as a metonym for men who are dark-skinned, dangerous, stupid and uncivilized. Tobin (2000: 81)

These early judgements are likely to affect children's later attitudes and behaviour. But the good news is that it is possible for them to unlearn what they have already learnt and to treat adults and children who are different from themselves respectfully and fairly. They can understand the concept of fairness and unfairness and appreciate that a wide range of physical features are beautiful.

Children learn from us how to behave, what we think is important and what we value. We are in a strong position to positively influence attitudes, challenge bias and enable children to stand up for themselves and others – but only if we understand how their own lives are affected by oppression and injustice. For example, children who experience racist discrimination may need our support to reinforce a strong group and personal identity and prevent their internalising the negative messages they receive from the world around them.

For large numbers of children their world is full of harsh realities and complex relationships and even children whose own lives are happy and secure are aware of and influenced by the injustice and discrimination that operates outside their immediate environment. The Dolls enable us to present children with an inclusive view of the world around them. The stories give them opportunities to see Black people, refugees (who may also be Black), Gypsies/Travellers and people with disabilities living happy and successful lives. Other stories describe difficulties and problems the Dolls experience that flow from the discrimination and prejudices they encounter. Children are empowered and encouraged to empathise and actively support the Dolls.

Adults and children in Britain and other European countries have for centuries been exposed to racist, sexist and other oppressive attitudes and practices. Young children currently receive both subtle and obvious messages suggesting that White customs, traditions and way of life are the 'right ones' and that it is 'better' to be male than female. But children are active participants in this learning process so the extent to which they absorb these messages will depend on a number of factors, such as their ethnicity, personality, social class, the attitudes and behaviour they witness in their homes and in the settings they attend. Iram Siraj-Blatchford and Priscilla Clarke (2000:5) believe that children's perceptions of themselves also play a part:

> ... every girl or disabled child does not perceive themselves in the same way. In fact, children from structurally disadvantaged groups often hold contradictory positions, which is why we might find in our classrooms black and other minority ethnic children who are very confident and academically successful in spite of the structural, cultural and interpersonal racism in society. Similarly, we will find working class boys who do not conform to a stereotype and are caring and unaggressive and African Caribbean boys who are capable and well-behaved.

The Persona Doll approach offers us an effective, stimulating, nonthreatening and enjoyable way to combat discrimination, foster empathy, raise equality issues and empower young children. Although oppressions form an overlapping and intersecting web, they are discussed here under separate headings.

Combating racism

It is widely believed that five White racists killed Stephen Lawrence. Their alleged involvement has implications for all of us and raises a number of questions about their childhood experiences. When they were young children were they given opportunities to unlearn any discriminatory messages they had already learnt?

- As young children, were they encouraged to empathise with and care about the Black children in their group and Black characters in books and stories?

- If they expressed racist comments or physically abused Black peers, were they helped to appreciate the consequences of their words and/or actions?

- Did they appear to resent and not understand when Black children who in their eyes were 'inferior', did better than they did?

- If their self-esteem seemed low, were efforts made to help them feel good about themselves? Children with a poor self-image are less likely to be able to put themselves in other people's shoes or to care about what happens to them.

- Did they attend settings where practitioners tried to ensure that racism did not blunt children's personal, social and emotional development but failed to make an impression?

- Did the racist input from parents and their community exert greater influence?

The Macpherson Report on the murder of Stephen Lawrence states that racism starts among the very young and becomes deeply ingrained. This claim is backed by David Milner (1983). He found that by the time they were 2 years old children notice differences in skin colour and that between 3 and 5 they have learnt from the world around them that it is 'better' to be White in Britain than Black.

Black children and White are damaged by racism, but in different ways. Many young Black children suffer abuse and rejection from their White peers, causing them to become angry and frustrated or depressed and withdrawn. Such feelings are compounded if adults fail to react positively. In racist societies like ours even the most supportive families find it difficult to counter the effects of negative and destructive experiences. Persona Dolls and their stories can boost Black children's confidence, self-esteem, identity formation and motivation to learn. Through the storytelling sessions we communicate our high expectations of each and every child, their right to be proud of their culture, their colour and their identity and we offer support to those experiencing discriminatory attitudes and behaviour.

As a consequence of racism, many White children develop feelings of superiority which may cause them to respond in an insensitive and uncaring way toward Black children and adults – a reaction which is likely to limit their ability to empathise and to sustain stable and meaningful relationships. When their Black peers achieve better results than they do, they might feel that their feelings of superiority and their self-esteem are under threat. Racism gives White children 'permission' to dislike Black children, physically abuse them and call them hurtful names. The Dolls and their stories challenge this licence by encouraging them to unlearn racist attitudes and behaviour. By celebrating diversity they are given the opportunity to value, respect and learn about a range of cultures, lifestyles and languages.

Many refugee children also experience racism. Immigration has been, and still is, used by politicians and the media to stereotype and scapegoat particular ethnic groups. A century ago, doors were often closed to Jews and others fleeing persecution and today we find the same acrimonious arguments, especially in the tabloids, being used to keep out people from Africa, Asia, Latin America and the Caribbean – countries previously colonised and exploited. Young children exposed to the media's whipping up of public opinion against refugees and asylum seekers run the risk of absorbing these derogatory views. Using refugee Persona Dolls with whom the children can identify and bond may, one hopes, help to reduce the impact of negative images and messages.

Those refugee children who are coping with the loss of parents, siblings, members of their extended family and friends as well as their home, favourite toys and pets may get support and security from the Dolls and simple stories that deal, for example, with loss.

For Gypsy/Traveller families racism is a fact of life. In view of their past and present experiences they steadfastly preserve their way of life and keep themselves to themselves. We need to ensure that the stories we tell accurately and respectfully reflect their lifestyle, acknowledge their fund of practical knowledge and first hand experience of, for example, plants and animals. These stories encourage children to respect and acknowledge the many positive aspects of Traveller life and need to be told whether or not we have Gypsy/Traveller children in the group. To ensure the Dolls represent Gypsy/Traveller communities accurately and appropriately, Traveller Education Support teams and parents need to be consulted.

Combating sexism

By the age of 3 both girls and boys have developed fixed ideas about the roles of men and women. By the time they are 5, many think that the female role is the one less valued and valuable. Many boys prefer to behave in ways that are traditionally associated with the male role and reject the qualities they have learnt to associate with the female role. Girls, on the other hand, behave in ways associated with both roles but see male roles as being more interesting and exciting. This way of thinking is challenged when both boy and girl Persona Dolls are shown to be powerful 'people'. During the storytelling session, sexist comments and behaviour are challenged in a firm but sensitive, non-threatening way. The Dolls and their stories have the potential to positively influence children's identity formation by breaking down stereotypes, widening girls' aspirations, fostering their curiosity about how things work, while encouraging boys to express their feelings, enjoy the discussions and develop concentration. The macho image that attracts so many young boys can be countered but Davies (1989) warns us that boys and girls often resist themes that challenge their own gender stereotypes and that they may 'read' non-traditional stories in very traditional ways.

Combating ableism

Negative attitudes to people with disabilities, like racist and sexist attitudes, are also deeply rooted. Children acquire them from adults, the media and the general way society is organised. The Dolls and the stories we tell can challenge this process and prevent them from perpetuating and reinforcing the cycle of discrimination when they grow up. The stories need to give non-disabled children accurate information, encourage them to ask questions and express their feelings. We need to help children with disabilities to handle and challenge name-calling, physical abuse and stereotypical attitudes. Teasing and bullying should not be allowed during circle or any other time. All the children should be able to feel safe and valued in the setting at all times. Storytelling sessions can indicate the terms people with disabilities prefer and the ones they find insulting and hurtful. Children can be encouraged to empathise and avoid unkind terms. The sessions provide an environment that actively encourages disabled and non-disabled children to interact with and learn from each other.

Combating homophobia

Persona Dolls and their stories also provide an effective way to combat assumptions about what is normal and natural sexual behaviour and to extend children's knowledge and understanding of the different ways in which families are structured. Children whose experience of family is different from the 'norm' may feel theirs is of less value and possibly even something to be ashamed of.

Many young children from heterosexual families have learnt that lesbian and gay lifestyles are unacceptable and although they may not understand what the terms like 'lezzy' mean, they know they have negative connotations. As Pogrebin (1980:12) points out:

> Before children have the vaguest ideas about who or what is a homosexual, they learn that homosexuality is something frightening, horrid, and nasty. They become homophobic long before they understand what it is they fear.

Today children increasingly use the term gay to describe something that isn't good. For example, 'That was a gay programme', means they thought it was bad. 'That bicycle is really gay' means that it is useless.

Tobin (2000) argues that class bias and homophobia embedded in films like *Swiss Family Robinson* feed on and reinforce pre-existing prejudices and anxieties.

> In group after group, children at Koa [elementary school] described the bad guys as the men without homes, nice clothes, good grooming, women or children. I find this worrisome on several counts – first, because it suggests a belief, which Disney and other filmmakers tap into, that poor people are dangerous to middle-class families; second, because it encourages fear and loathing for the homeless, who tend to be portrayed in the news as hordes of men without women and children; and third, because in the equation of womanless and childless men with danger, I perceive the workings of homophobia. Bad guys in Disney animated films are often effeminate. ... Effeminacy aside, the suggestion that men who don't live in families are dangerous to children is a pernicious fiction in the morally panicked, homophobic era in which we live. ...The reality is that very few abusers are gay men, or men living alone. Tobin (2000:134-135)

Through the stories and the discussions we facilitate we need constantly to check that the language we use is not homophobic, that we challenge hurtful comments and name-calling and encourage children to use the terms lesbian and gay positively and appropriately. Like all parents, lesbian and gay parents have the right to expect their families to be valued and their children protected from abuse. By incorporating similarities and differences in family routines and practices like meal times and going to bed in the stories and then talking about them helps children appreciate that there are different but equally valid ways of being in a family.

Combating poverty

Poverty is embedded in our class-based society. According to the National Office of Statistics report published in May 2000, about three million children are living below the poverty line. When researching for a local authority in the north of England, Helen Penn was told by some of the mothers that poverty meant::

> Being so poor you bought your clothes from the £1 rail at charity shops; you could never afford a proper haircut; you had to plan an outing to the local swimming pool like a day trip to the seaside, saving and making arrangements weeks in advance; you worried about paying 60p for a loaf of bread and you were afraid when the holidays came

because there were no free school dinners. (*Nursery World* 13th January 2000:10).

As individuals we can not alter the fact that many children are born into poverty, live in poverty and die in poverty but we can provide a supportive, safe and stimulating environment for them. Through our Persona Dolls stories we can offer them hopeful and empowering experiences and images so they do not feel overwhelmed and discouraged. And, very importantly, we can help challenge any negative attitudes of the children growing up in more affluent families. Young children's comments show that they differentiate between rich and poor adults and children by the clothes they wear, the houses they live in and by their possessions, even though they might not understand the concepts of wealth and poverty. Superior and patronising attitudes develop from an early age. The stories counter the message that rich people are 'better' and happier than poor people and encourage and support children who express egalitarian ideas, like 'I don't think it is fair that some people have more money than others'.

Researching with Persona Dolls

The Australian Preschool Equity and Social Diversity research project led by Dr Glenda MacNaughton uses Persona Dolls to uncover young children's prejudices and discriminatory attitudes and to promote a sense of fairness and justice. Space is devoted to describing this research here because it draws on one-to-one interviews with children and their recorded responses to the Dolls. It enables us to hear from the children themselves what they think and feel about themselves and other people. This is important because, as Cannella (1998:10) says, '*The most critical voices that are silent in our constructions of early childhood education are the children with whom we work. Our constructions of research have not fostered methods that facilitate hearing their voices.*'

The aims of MacNaughton's project are:

- to find out what 4 and 5 year-old children knew about 'race', class and gender when she and her co-researcher first met them

- to use the Dolls and their stories to positively introduce a range of equity and social diversity issues to the children

- to evaluate if and how the Dolls and their stories changed what the children knew.

The children were interviewed and asked semi-structured questions. Four Persona Dolls acting, as ice-breakers, helped to keep the children's conversations focused and provided opportunities for the researchers to tell stories around class, 'race' and gender issues. The children were encouraged to play with the Dolls:

Shiree, from an Aboriginal-Australian family

Willie, from a Vietnamese-Australian family

Olivia, from a rich Anglo-Australian family and

Tom, from a poor Anglo-Australian family.

MacNaughton's focus is on comparing and exploring the differences and similarities between the silences and voices of 4 and 5 year-old Anglo-Australian and Vietnamese-Australian children. Her approach is based on the work of Jonathon Silin who suggests that:

Silence can signal resistance as well as oppression, voice can create new moments for social control as well as for personal efficacy. And words are notorious for concealing and transforming as well as revealing the truth of our lives. (Silin 1999:44)

The co-researcher in the project, Heather, had the ability to wait patiently for children to answer her questions. Instead of jumping to the conclusion that their lack of response always signified indifference, shyness or ignorance, she read the silence which often greeted her questions to mean that they were thinking hard about what she had asked them. The following exchange captures how valuing silences can elicit important information about how young children think about the complex issues of diversity.

Researcher: I'm just wondering what you know about Aboriginal people. 'Cause you noticed when you came in that this was a different doll, didn't you? You noticed that ... [LONG PAUSE WAITING FOR CHILD]

Jane: And, sometimes they make houses and sometimes they move on, because um they make it out of sticks and leaves. And also Aboriginals will
[VERY LONG PAUSE/STOPS].

Researcher: Anything else you can think of about Aboriginals that you know about?

Jane: Nope. And sometimes Aboriginals also um they also
um Aboriginals
[PAUSE].

Researcher: What about you? Do you know anybody Aboriginal? Do you know any Aboriginal people?

Jane: Two.

Researcher: You know two. Oh I see.

Jane: Boory and ah Bill Hiney.

Researcher: And where do they live?

Jane: Um they live in Melbourne.

Researcher: They live in Melbourne.
[LONG PAUSE WAITING FOR CHILD TO CONTINUE]

Jane: But I also know that um a long, long time ago that the white people um took their children, the Aboriginal children away their mum and dad because they thought that they weren't treating them well. And also I think
[PAUSE – HEATHER WAITS]

Researcher: Anything else? You're trying so hard to remember. We'll talk about something else and if you happen to remember anything that you wanted to say you can just tell me. Okay. Now let's look at these dolls. Can you tell me something that looks different about these dolls?

Jane: That one is brown and that one is white.

Researcher: Anything else that's different?

Jane: The eyes are different? And she doesn't have [UNCLEAR], and they have different hair. They have different clothes, different skin.

Heather's patience encouraged Jane to reveal to the researchers that she knew more about Aboriginal people than she first expressed. They would not have known that she knew anything about the 'stolen generations' or about her attempts to make sense of this. The 'stolen generations' were the Aboriginal children who were force-fully removed from their families because it was believed that they would have better life-chances if they were raised in White Australian homes. MacNaughton believes that although Jane's knowledge is uncertain, she is working hard to construct meanings about Aboriginal people and their lives in the past and in the here and now. The meanings she is giving to the word Aboriginal also shows that young children can develop understandings of complex contemporary issues and show empathy for the pain of others. There is much that can be added to her understandings but at 4 she has already learnt that there is more to being Aboriginal than skin colour.

However, most of the Anglo-Australian children's understandings about Aboriginal Australians were misunderstandings and many children knew little or nothing about these indigenous peoples and their culture. Common to those children who did have some know-ledge were the beliefs that 'they' lived a long time ago and that 'they' were strange or exotic in some way. This was most clearly illustrated by the way the children reacted to Shiree, the Doll from the Aboriginal Australian family. One child asked 'Why does that Doll have clothes on?' Another was afraid of her and pointed to Shiree, telling the researchers to 'put that Doll away'. Several of the children didn't want to talk about her or look at her, saying that they wanted to play with Tom and/or Olivia.

Identifying with the Dolls

Prompted by questions from the researchers, the children in this study talked willingly about which Dolls looked most like them and the differences they could see between them.

Researcher: Can you notice anything that is different about these Dolls?

Child: That one (Willie) and that one (Shiree) haven't got the same coloured skin.

Researcher Can you tell me what colour their skin is? Do you have some words for that?

Child: Black and a kind of greenish colour.

Researcher: What about the other Dolls, what words would you use for the colour of those Dolls?

Child: That one is white (Olivia) and so is that one (Tom).

The focus on Shiree's skin colour by the Anglo-Australian children was also associated with uncertainty and discomfort. At times, a few of them actively rejected her (6–14%). Most often this discomfort and rejection was conveyed through powerful silences. Some of the children's responses to questions about Shiree were accompanied by a strong verbal or physical refusal to touch or hold her. Sally expressed this simply and powerfully:

Researcher: This one is Shiree. Would you like to hold her?

Sally: No yuk.

Sally had wanted to hold each of the other Dolls.

The Vietnamese-Australian children tended to self-identify with Olivia or Tom rather than with Willie, as Heather's interview with Vietnamese-Australian Kim illustrates. The centre that Kim attends is strongly committed to bilingualism and her teacher believed that Kim spoke sufficient English to participate in the project. Kim held tightly onto Heather's hand when she entered the room. Her attention quickly fixed on the Dolls. She sat down and listened attentively and looked closely at each one as they were introduced to her. Heather explained that she was going to ask Kim some questions.

Heather: Do you understand, Kim?

Kim: NODS

Heather:	When you look at the Dolls can you tell me which Doll you think looks most like you?
Kim:	SILENCE. SHE LOOKS AT HEATHER THEN CASTS HER EYES DOWN AND POINTS AT OLIVIA. SHE BLUSHES VERY STRONGLY AS SHE DOES SO.
Heather:	I see. Can you take a good look for me and be sure.
Kim:	NODS AND THEN POINTS AGAIN AT OLIVIA THIS TIME HOLDING HEATHER'S GAZE. SHE BLUSHES AGAIN.

Kim was silent but responded clearly and unambiguously. Her non-verbal communication conveyed that she looked like Olivia, (the Doll from a rich Anglo-Australian family) and not like any of the other Dolls. This was particularly interesting given that later in the interview she identified facial and skin tones as the main differences she could see between the Dolls. Her blushes suggest that she knew that the researchers knew that she knew she didn't look like Olivia.

All the Vietnamese-Australian children remained silent about their reasons for self-identifying with a particular Doll except one little girl. She pointed to Willie '... *because this one skin most like me*'. Like Kim, they too commented on skin colour when identifying differences between the Dolls. Half of them identified skin and face colour as the first and main difference between the Dolls.

MacNaughton compared these self-identification comments and silences about skin tone with a moment of 'voice' and silence in an interview with James, a four year-old Anglo-Australian child.

Researcher:	Well this is Olivia and this is the last of the Dolls you will meet today. Is there anything you can tell me about Olivia?
James:	She is very pretty.
Researcher:	What makes her pretty?
Researcher:	What's that you are pointing at, her dress? Is there anything else that makes her pretty?
James:	This does.

Researcher: What's that, can you use your words to tell me?

James: Legs, these are knees.

James: LOOKS AT OLIVIA'S FACE VERY CLOSELY FOR SEVERAL SECONDS.

PICKING UP ON THIS CUE, THE RESEARCHER ASKED:

Researcher: What about her face, is there anything about her face you can tell me?

James: Her face is lovely like mine because it's lighter. It's like Tom's.

James clearly expressed his opinion about Olivia's loveliness but when asked about Willie he was silent. Like the majority of Anglo-Australian children interviewed (42/44) he offered no comment on the word 'Vietnamese'. In fact, only two Anglo-Australian children responded to questions about being Vietnamese. One said that Vietnamese people have 'a strange name' and 'shop in markets', the other that they have 'yellow faces' and 'black hair'. MacNaughton notes that layered into Anglo-Australian children's silences about Willie and about being Vietnamese were comments that Willie was 'not Australian'; being Australian meant to them having 'white' skin. The children also said that:

'Willie couldn't be Australian because even though he was born in Australia he is still Vietnamese.'

'Willie and Shiree are not Australian because 'they've got different faces.'

'Willie and Shiree must ask God if they want to be Australian. God might allow Shiree to be Australian but not Willie.'

Uncovering the thinking behind the words

The researchers quickly realised that it was important to ask children why they thought what they did. One of Olivia's stories, called 'The Blue Badge', illustrates the point.

In this story Olivia is given a badge for her birthday that has a 5 on it. It is a Blue Badge. She is so excited by the badge that she wears it to her day nursery and shows her friends. They laugh at her and say it can't really be her badge because it's blue. At this point in the story the children are asked:

'Do you think that Olivia's friends are right?'

The reply in unison from the eight children listening to the story is 'no'.

Heather asks: 'Why?'.

'Well, girls and boys can wear any colour they like,' comes the response in unison once again.

It is clear that the children have been told this regularly by the staff.

Heather then asks, 'Why do you think that Olivia's friends said what they did?'

The response back: 'Because well, pink's really for girls and blue is really for boys'.

Skin colour matters

Of the twenty four (56%) children who gave a reason for their choice of Doll to self-identify with 38% of the Anglo-Australian children cited skin colour. The fact that skin colour contributes to how they self-identify and how they identify others is demonstrated in this conversation between Jamie, an Anglo-Australian little girl, and the researcher.

Researcher: This is Shiree, is there anything you can tell me about Shiree?

Researcher: No. Does she look like Olivia? What's the same? Can you use words for me?

Jamie: Curly hair.

Researcher: What about the colour of her hair? Can you tell me about that?

Jamie: It's not the same.

Researcher: What's different? Can you use some words to tell me?

Jamie: Their socks.

Researcher: Their socks are different, what about their faces, if you have a look at their faces?

Jamie Their colour is different.

Researcher: Their colour is very different, what words would you use to describe their colour?

Jamie: I don't know.

Researcher: What about the colour of her hair, what colour would that be?

Jamie: Black.

Researcher: And if you look at her face, what colour is her face?

Jamie: Brown.

Researcher: What about Olivia, what colour is Olivia's face?

Jamie: White.

Researcher: What about your face? What colour is your face?

Jamie: White too.

Researcher: So, your face is a bit like Olivia's face. Do you know anybody who has a face like Shiree? The colour of Shiree? Have you ever met anyone?

Jamie: No.

Researcher: Well, Shiree is from an Aboriginal family, do you know any Aboriginal people?

Jamie: No.

Researcher: Have you heard about Aboriginal people?

Jamie: Yes.

Researcher: Can you tell me anything about them? What have you heard about them?

Jamie: I heard that they have the same colour as this.

Researcher: Have you heard anything else about them?

Jamie: Just that they are black.

Anglo-Australian children also used 'whiteness' as a category when deciding which Doll looked most like them and when discussing Shiree. One child's *only comment* during her interview was in response to the question, 'Which Doll looks most like you?' Pointing to Olivia she said, 'I'm white'.

MacNaughton suggests that the children's reactions were consistent with research by, *inter alia*, Aboud and Doyle (1995) which showed that White children are often negatively biased against Black children. It might be useful to reflect on some of the questions posed by MacNaughton in relation to children in our own settings and how they might react especially if, like most of the children in the study, they have had little or no exposure to Persona Dolls.

- Some young children sort people by physical attributes such as skin colour rather than by other equally obvious differences produced by gender or clothes. Why do many not do this?

- What makes physical characteristics such as skin colour that have historically been named as 'racial' so prominent in young children's classifications?

- Did the Vietnamese-Australian girls really believe that they looked like Olivia?

- Were Kim and the other Vietnamese-Australian girls merely mistaken about their appearance when they chose Olivia?

- Were the Vietnamese-Australian children resisting the efforts to classify them?

- What was Kim revealing or concealing?

- Were the Anglo-Australian children showing racial bias?

- Why was Shiree the most rejected Doll and Olivia the only one described as pretty?

In summary

MacNaughton believes that Persona Dolls, their stories and the conversations they initiate can and do illuminate the diverse and complex understandings young children are constructing about the social world around them. She emphasises the importance of using Persona Dolls with skill and sensitivity and that the storytelling process has to go hand-in-hand with the process of listening to children in a spirit of commitment to fairness and respect for all those involved. She suggests that success in helping children learn to respect diversity and unlearn unfairness is most likely when practitioners:

• ask children what they know about social diversity

• allow children time to reflect on the issues practitioners are discussing with them and be patient in seeking their answers to our questions

• develop conversations by seeking the reasons behind the answers they give

• prepare the children for small group discussion

• evaluate progress.

This research confirms that Persona Dolls and their stories are a powerful tool for practising anti-bias work with young children. They excite children's interest, they fascinate adults and they intrigue parents. The researchers learnt that:

• good organization and preparation is essential

• The capacity to wait and listen to someone else talking is essential to achieving the goals associated with the Persona Doll process.

• group dynamics can undermine and/or illuminate the work

• the most powerfully remembered stories and dolls are those that link with the children's existing knowledge base

• that gender is an important factor in how children attend to and remember the dolls and their stories

- children have complex understandings of equity and social diversity issues and they can be helped to build respect and learn about unfairness through the dolls and their stories.

The publication of the completed research will make fascinating reading. I hope it will trigger similar Persona Doll research to uncover the attitudes of young British children.

It seems reasonable to assume that if children are offered rich and diverse cultural experiences, are helped to develop a strong sense of fairness and are empowered, they are more likely as adults to fight for change and against inequality. Persona Dolls and their stories contribute to this process.

4

A different kind of storytelling

In this chapter the key points that distinguish Persona Doll stories from other stories are identified and the part played by the practitioner and the children during storytelling sessions is outlined. The chapter ends with suggestions on how to present the stories and to evaluate the sessions.

Storytelling is a powerful way of communicating with children because stories are magical for them. Throughout history, parents and grandparents have used storytelling to pass on family and cultural information from generation to generation. It is a technique that is used by practitioners in many settings. Well-told stories captivate children and help them develop an understanding of narrative, become more fluent, extend their vocabularies and have the language to talk about their emotions, experiences and ideas.

Persona Doll stories are special. They are woven around the Dolls who visit the setting at circle time or at a special small group time. Through the stories children learn accurate and authentic details about each Doll – its family, cultural background, its personality. Their identification and bonding with the Dolls deepens as more and more stories are told about them. The Dolls and their stories reflect the hopes and fears, successes and failures, of the children. Like all stories, Persona Doll stories have a beginning but they do not have the customary middle and end. The practitioner sets the scene by telling the children the incident the Doll wants to share with them – rather like presenting a scenario. The children are then encouraged to identify the Doll's feelings, empathise with it, express their opinions and help solve its problem. Drawing on experiences, feelings, family relationships and other details from the children's own lives can intensify their identification with the Doll and their involvement in the story. Interesting contexts help to make the stories realistic, capture children's attention and arouse their emotions. Consequently, most stories are based on children's experiences – happy and painful – within the setting, in their homes and outside it, like celebrating birthdays, going on holiday, or being excluded from play, teased and bullied.

Stories can help children to learn coping skills and to appreciate that they are not the only ones who experience certain feelings. Children have to learn how to identify emotions and have the words to describe them before they can put themselves in the Doll's shoes and empathise with it. They need opportunities to talk about their feelings. They can be encouraged to say how they feel when they are frightened, when they were really happy, when they are worried, when they are upset, when people make supportive comments and when nasty remarks are made about them.

Louise Derman-Sparks (1989:19) quotes Kay Taus, the pioneer of the concept of using Persona Dolls to confront bias: '*A second source of stories are current hot world events that appear on the news or are talked about by parents.*' Stories can help to counter the prejudices and misinformation children pick up from adult conversations about, for instance, refugees. Children whose parents are unemployed might welcome stories around Dolls whose parents are out of work. The stories can promote understanding and empathy in children whose parents are working. The Dolls and their stories can also address children's fears triggered by TV pictures of natural disasters and war.

The third source from which Taus draws are stories about people and events in the struggle for justice and freedom in America, such as Harriet Tubman and Rosa Parks. She shares her own involvement in the Civil Rights Movement with children. She doesn't expect them to remember all the details, '... *but I do want to give them a sense of the great many people like themselves who have reflected a spirit of justice and freedom*'.

Stories about the history of resistance challenge the myth that Black people, women and people with disabilities were or are passive victims. When we draw on the lives of people with whom children identify we can inspire them and deepen their understanding of and commitment to combating injustice. Although these stories are not woven around the Dolls, we could let them join the circle and 'listen' to the stories with the children. The Dolls could 'tell' stories about members of their families of whom they are proud because they changed or are changing the conditions under which people live. The children may have parents and grandparents who actively partici-pated or still participate in trade union activities or liberation struggles or who remember discriminatory incidents from their childhood. They could be invited to come and tell their stories. A Black parent told this story to the children in Vivian Paley's class:

> Once when I was little, Martin Luther King, Jr., came to speak at our church. It was a long speech and I don't remember most of it, but there was something he told us about his daughter Yolanda that I never forgot... When Yolanda was young, her daddy was always being invited everywhere to give speeches. And she liked going with him to the airport. They always drove past a big amusement park... the rides seemed wonderful to Yolanda. Every time they drove by she asked her father if he would take her there when he came back from his trip. And when she asked him he looked uncomfortable and said, 'Yolanda, honey, I'll try my best,' but he never took her. Well, this happened again and again and one day Yolanda burst out crying and she couldn't stop, she was that unhappy. They had been on their way home from the airport and she knew there was time to go on the rides. She was still crying when they got home.

> Her daddy realized he had to tell her the truth. So he sat her on his lap and said, 'Yolanda, honey, there is a reason your mother and I can't take you to Playland. And it is a very mean reason because it makes a little girl like you cry.'

> Yolanda looked at her father with her big dark eyes and asked, 'What's the reason, daddy?'

> 'They won't let you go on the rides because you're Black. Those rides are only for White children. I hadn't wanted to tell you this.'

Yolanda wasn't crying any more. She was trying to figure out what her father meant. Finally she said, 'Then I don't like those rides.' Dr King hugged his daughter and smiled at her. 'It's okay to like those rides, honey, and it's okay to want to go on them. Those people are wrong, not you. But, baby, listen to me. Even if you can't go to Playland, you're just as good as all the children who can go. Not one of those kids is nicer or better than you!'

... [Yolanda is] a grown woman now. She can take her children there [to Playland] whenever she wants to. (Paley 1995: 24-25)

Telling children about any discriminatory experiences we faced when we were children can provide a valuable learning experience for them but only if we feel comfortable talking about what happened.

The role of the adult

We start the storytelling session by setting the scene. With the Doll on our lap, we tell the children in an everyday speaking voice what the Doll has come to tell them about a particular experience, situation or feeling. We then adopt the role of facilitator. We encourage the children to do most of the talking and listen carefully and actively to each child's contributions, trigger discussion and offer support when necessary. Being a good facilitator requires sensitivity, perceptiveness, flexibility and openness; ensuring that children's opinions are valued and respected, that no child is humiliated when expressing her/his beliefs and that everyone participates in a supportive and sensitive way. As Tobin (2000:22) notes:

We can never know exactly, precisely, confidently what another person is feeling or thinking from what he or she says. The best we can do is to listen empathetically, think about what he has said to us, and then answer.

During the storytelling sessions we need to appreciate that there are cultural differences in what is considered to be an acceptable physical distance between one person and another. We also need to be aware that the body language young children from different ethnic and cultural backgrounds are learning might be different from our own. For example, if we have learnt to associate looking 'straight-in-the-eye' with frankness and honesty we run the risk of misinterpreting children's non-verbal communication. Many Black children are taught that to do so is disrespectful and impolite whereas White children are taught to look directly at an adult when they are spoken to. Partington and McCudden (1992:221) draw our attention to the fact that verbal communication is governed by cultural rules. Ignoring these can result in *different speakers being accused of rudeness, even though they are operating within a set of culturally accepted rules: but they are the rules of another culture*. As the range of differences that exist within and between cultures is so great we need to avoid simplistic, stereotypical assumptions about the way a child from a particular cultural group is likely to respond.

The language we use, the activities we provide and the way we present them may reflect the home experiences of some of the children but be unfamiliar to others. Before adding a resource that is unfamiliar to all or some of the children it might be an idea to tell a Persona Doll story that includes its correct name, the way it is used and what it is used for. This could extend children's vocabularies and general knowledge and help to counter prejudice and misinformation and, ideally, limit offensive remarks and behaviour.

During the storytelling sessions we need to be careful that we accept and acknowledge that some children's ideas about the 'right' way to act and interact will not match ours and to keep checking that we don't unconsciously respond more positively to the children who are most like us.

> As professionals, teachers must develop ways to learn about, and understand, children's cultures and the language of learning in their homes. They must work jointly with parents and children – teaching them and learning from them – to combine styles of everyday language use with language styles used for learning and inquiry at home and in school. (Dinah Volk 1997:60)

We also need to ensure that we use appropriate terms to describe ethnic, cultural, linguistic and physical diversity. For example, when describing ethnic diversity, physical characteristics like hair and facial features should be included. Adopting an anti-discriminatory approach includes describing differences in a positive way – neither denying them nor using negative labels and language. But we might use certain terms without realising they can cause offence since preferred terms change over time depending on the way adults and children in particular groups are being perceived and how they perceive themselves. Consequently, preferred terms change as conditions and perceptions change. This is how an African American teacher explained the term Black to a class of Black children and White:

> ... words can make you feel wonderful or terrible, strong or weak, ugly or pretty. 'Black' is one of those words that over the years has been very sensitive for black people... Before 1960 it wasn't beautiful to be black. Our black hair was not beautiful, our black skin, our black noses, nothing about black was beautiful, not even among ourselves... In the middle of the sixties and seventies we black people began to realise we had a lot to be proud of and that black was not ugly, it was beautiful. That's why I still use it, in addition to African American. Once it became beautiful I wanted it to stay beautiful. (Vivian Paley 1995:118)

To avoid using insulting and degrading terms we need constantly to check with the adults and children concerned – to ask them how would they like us to refer to the group(s) to which they belong and to any impairments they may have.

MacNaughton(1994) stresses the role that gender plays:

> Gender needs to be understood as a way of being, thinking, experiencing and feeling that drives and influences development. Children's gender influences every aspect of their development, from their values, beliefs, language, emotion, imagination, cognition and style of communication to their involvement in physical activities, use of space and social relationships... It is also important to be aware of what specific aspects of the gender factor in children's development need to be challenged and/or supported through an anti-bias curriculum.

When presenting Persona Dolls, creating scenarios and facilitating group discussion we need to be aware of any gender stereotypes we have in our heads so that we can expand and not limit children's view of what it means to be a boy and to be a girl. They will be influenced by the way we speak and behave and by the stories we create.

For example we need to check whether we:

- frequently refer to doctors as 'he' and nurses as 'she', or describe boys in terms of their skill and girls in terms of their looks

- support and encourage girls and boys to adopt non-traditional gender roles

- encourage children through our Persona Doll stories to think of boys and girls as active leaders

- reinforce girls' and boys' self-esteem and pride in their gender identity.

Understanding that it is their anatomical differences that make them male or female helps children recognise that they will still be girls if they climb trees and still be boys if they play with dolls – that having or not having a penis doesn't affect their ability to build with bricks, play tea-parties or dress up in frilly clothes! Through the Persona Doll storytelling sessions we can encourage children to think about questions like whether it is fair that boys miss out on some toys and activities and girls on others.

If we continually monitor our response to individual children during storytelling sessions we increase the likelihood of treating each one equally and with equal concern. If, for example, there is only one child with a disability in the group, we need to keep a watchful eye on her/his reactions especially when telling a story about a Doll with a disability. By equally praising, acknowledging and responding positively to all children's contributions we actively boost their confidence and self-esteem – their picture of their strengths and weaknesses. Jenny Mosley (1993) reminds us that:

> If children hear regular good news about their qualities and strengths, they are more able to work constructively on improving their weaknesses. ... (others) hear the 'good news' as well and correspondingly think and respond more positively toward that individual.

Treating some children less favourably than others can be a subtle process, as Cecile Wright's participant study reveals. She found that many White practitioners unconsciously expected bad behaviour from African-Caribbean children, especially from the boys, who were consequently discouraged and constantly criticised and disapproved of. This example recorded by Wright (1991:28) refers to four year old Marcus, the only African-Caribbean boy in the group:

Teacher: Let's do one song before home time.

Peter: Humpty Dumpty.

Teacher: No, I'm choosing today. Let's do something we have not done for a while. I know, we'll do the Autumn song. Don't shout out, put your hands up nicely.

Mandy (shouting out) Two little leaves on a tree.

Teacher: She's nearly right.

Marcus: (with his hand up) I know.

Teacher: (talking to the group) Is she right when she says two little leaves on a tree?

Whole group: No.

Teacher: What is it Peter?

Peter: Four.

Teacher: Nearly right.

Marcus: (waving his hand for attention) Five.

Teacher: Don't shout out Marcus, do you know Susan?

Susan: Five.

Teacher: (holding up one hand) Good, five, because we have got how many fingers on this hand?

Whole group: Five.

Teacher: OK, let's only have one hand because we've only got five leaves. How many would we have if we had too many? Don't shout out, hands up.

Mandy:	(shouting out) One, two, three. Four, five, six, seven, eight, nine, ten.
Teacher:	Good. OK how many fingers have we got?
Marcus:	Five.
Teacher:	Don't shout out Marcus, put your hand up. Deane, how many?
Deane:	Five.
Teacher:	That's right, we're going to use five today, what makes them dance about?
Peter:	(Shouting out) The wind.
Teacher:	That's right, ready, here we go.

Teacher and children sing: Five little leaves so bright and gay, dance about on a tree one day. The wind came blowing through the town, whooo, whooo, one little leaf came tumbling down.

Teacher:	How many have we got left?
Deane:	(shouting out) One.
Marcus:	(raising his hand enthusiastically) Four.
Teacher:	(to Marcus) Shush. Let's count, one two, three, four. How many Deane?
Deane:	Four.
Teacher:	Good, right, let's do the next bit.

Teacher and children sing the next two verses.

Teacher:	How many have we got left, Peter?
Peter:	Don't know.
Mandy:	Two.
Teacher:	I know you know, Mandy.
Marcus:	Two.

Teacher:	(stern voice) I'm not asking you, I'm asking Peter, don't shout out. We'll help Peter, shall we? Look at my fingers, how many? One, two. How many Peter?
Peter:	Two.
Teacher:	Very good. Let's do the next bit.

Teacher and children sing the next verse and at the end of it:

Teacher:	How many have we got left, Susan?
Susan:	One
Teacher:	Good, let's all count, one. Let's do the last bit.

Teacher and children sing the last verse and at the end:

Teacher:	How many have we got left?
Whole group:	None.
Teacher:	That's right, there are no leaves left. Marcus, will you stop fidgeting and sit nicely.

In a conversation about this observation, the African-Caribbean nursery nurse attached to the unit commented:

> Marcus really likes answering questions about things. I can imagine he's quite good at that because he's always got plenty to say ... but they [white teachers] see the black children as a problem here.

We can use Persona Dolls and their stories to counter unfair and discriminatory behaviour that Black children like Marcus experience in their daily lives. We can support and empower them to develop the skills they need to challenge their unfair treatment and empower the rest of the group to support and stand up for them.

Children who are at the early stages of learning English as an additional language might find Persona Doll storytelling sessions difficult to cope with because the Doll sitting on the practitioner's lap provides them with few visual clues. Their discomfort could be eased if practitioners, parents or somebody from the community was at hand to translate the stories and any contributions the children might like to make. If this is not possible then keywords from the children's languages could be woven into the stories. Not an easy option in a group in which there are several children whose home languages differ from one another, all learning English as an additional language.

To counter the possibility of fluent English speakers adopting superior attitudes towards children who are less fluent than they are, practitioners need to provide a multilingual environment that encourages all the children to know about and respect the full range of languages and the people who speak them. Stories and discussions that acknowledge and praise children clever enough to speak more than one language can have a positive effect.

Questioning children to spark ideas and reveal attitudes

Skilful questioning fosters children's self esteem and ensures that the rest of the group values their contributions, but much depends on how we ask the questions and the kind of questions we ask. This is how the teacher in this incident described by Faber and Mazlish (1996:190) responded to Charlene, a little girl who finds learning difficult.

> Charlene put up her hand during a story about a bee keeper and asked,
>
> 'Do a bee be a bird?'.
>
> The rest of the children were electrified. Several raised their hands and eagerly waved them about. The teacher said, 'Wait a minute children. Charlene, that is such an interesting question! What makes you think a bee could be a bird?'
>
> Very solemnly Charlene replied, 'They both got wings.'
>
> 'Is there anything else the same?'
>
> 'They fly.'
>
> 'You noticed two things that were the same. Class, is there anything that makes birds different from bees?
>
> 'Birds got feathers.'

'Birds is bigger.'

'Birds don't sting you.'

Suddenly Charlene's face lit up.

'I know, I know,' she called out. 'A bee is an INCEST!'

All the heads nodded.

On the board the teacher wrote the children's conclusion: A bee is an insect.

During a Persona Doll story about friendship, the questions we ask may reveal children's positive attitudes as well as their prejudices and stereotypical thinking.

• How do you know someone is your friend?

• Can someone be a friend when they are different from you?

• How do you choose your friends?

• How do you feel when your friends want to play with you?

• How do you feel when your friends don't want to play with you?

Open-ended questioning like this elicits information and encourages children to think about issues and express their feelings. But asking closed questions tends to increase the power of the adult and reduce children's spontaneity and willingness to express their true feelings and views. From their study of adult/child interaction styles in eight multi-ethnic nursery schools Ogilvy and others (1992) found that the number of questions and the way the teachers asked them put the Asian children under pressure. The teachers had a more controlling style when relating to them and although the White Scottish children were asked many questions, the Asian children were asked significantly more.

Cultural factors might be influencing children's responses. In most European cultures there is a strong sense of turn-taking associated with questioning – somebody asks a question and waits for an answer. We need to be aware that silences can speak volumes, as Lynch and Hanson (1992:233) explain:

> On the one hand, maintaining silence in a conversation may serve as an expression of interest and respect. On the other hand, if silence follows consistent verbal responses ... it may indicate disagreement or negative reactions such as anger.

Their emphasis on noting children's silences as well as their answers is echoed in the research approach adopted by MacNaughton and described in chapter three.

Children play a crucial role

Persona Doll storytelling sessions only work if children actively participate – freely expressing their opinions, emotions and thoughts. So it is essential that they are accustomed to having stories read and told to them, are able to listen to other children's opinions and to wait their turn before offering their contributions. In some settings a 'talking' object is passed around so that only the child who has the object in her/his hand can speak – though nobody has to talk if they don't want to.

Sessions seem to work best with small groups so everyone has the opportunity to be involved. In a large group children are likely to get restless waiting for their turn to speak and it might be more difficult for practitioners to keep track of how each one is feeling, who is contributing and who is not. It is important that everybody should, as far as possible, sit on the same level because, as Mosely (1993) says, 'the circle is a symbol of unity, wholeness and harmony'. If children who are wheelchair users are able to sit on chairs or on the floor the rest of the group should be seated accordingly. Children with hearing impairments need to be given as many visual clues as possible, while opportunities for touching are likely to benefit those who have visual impairments.

Children need to know that they will not be laughed at or teased, that their contributions will be listened to and that they will be treated as valuable members of the group. To ensure that everyone is clear about the responsibilities they have towards each other, ground rules need to be developed and periodically reviewed. This could be a useful small group activity to do with the children. It involves defining what each rule means and considering what would need to be done to ensure that it is implemented, and what we would need to do to make sure that everyone is listened to. Rules could include telling the truth, listening to each other, showing respect, caring for each other's feelings. Expressing these as do's instead of don'ts is likely to have more effect.

Although children are encouraged to participate as much as possible, to share their experiences and ideas and to listen to each other without interrupting, some may be reluctant to talk about their family and way of life. For example, refugee parents who have come from repressive societies, and Gypsy/Traveller parents who fiercely protect their culture from the prying eyes of outsiders, may have taught their children not to tell anybody anything about themselves or their families. We need to reassure parents and to explain that participating in the discussions will help their children achieve the Early Learning Goals. Once children bond with the Dolls they will probably offer information but until this happens we shouldn't press them.

The children's first task is to name the Doll's feelings, empathise with it and help and advise it. Those children who are experiencing similar problems are likely to believe that the Doll understands their feelings. They will probably be keen to advise it and may at the same time be learning to deal with their own problems. This can be especially helpful for refugee children who have been through traumatic experiences – they may discover their own strengths through solving the Dolls' problems.

The process of discussing feelings, ideas and solutions is more important than finding a perfect solution. Children who believe in themselves and trust others are likely to be able to identify and communicate with their peer group and the Dolls. They can share and extend their knowledge, understanding and enjoyment and boost their self-esteem and confidence. But some children in the group may be too angry, unhappy and confused to be able to participate constructively. They may be aggressive and disruptive or withdrawn and unresponsive. The strategies we adopt will depend on their individual circumstances and on the availability of other practitioners. Including their particular interests or hobbies in the stories might trigger their participation.

To be able to express their feelings and to empathise with the feelings of others, children need to have words in their vocabularies that describe positive and negative feelings. Storytelling sessions provide opportunities for them to name and talk about their own feelings and recall how they felt in particular situations.

Encouraging them to talk about themselves and their families provides opportunities for everyone to learn about the similarities and differences within the group. They can compare their own skin colour, hair and physical features with the other children's, the ways in which their family and cultural background are similar to and different from their friends, and the things they are able and unable to do. Using a variety of appropriate Persona Dolls with which to tell stories ensures that we present a wide range of equally valued and respected lifestyles, cultures, languages and abilities. Children can begin to appreciate that everybody is different, that nobody is exactly the same as anyone else, that it's good to be different and it isn't something to tease or harass each other about. This learning needs to be reinforced by supporting, respecting and reflecting the family and cultural backgrounds of all the children, both in the curriculum and in the resources provided.

The Dolls give children opportunities to notice, talk about and enjoy diversity while appreciating that people see and understand things differently. This can help them value diversity. Stories around Dolls with whom children have identified can reduce ridicule and feelings of superiority while promoting self-respect and pride. Children are able to feel good about themselves and their own culture(s) and at the same time respect other children and appreciate their cultures. If there are children who seem to us to feel bad about some aspect of themselves, hearing stories in which a Doll shows that it is comfortable with or proud of these aspects might encourage them to see themselves in a new light.

Begin at the beginning

We start by presenting the Doll to the children. We need to tell them why we are going to be talking for the Doll. We could explain that we are speaking for the Doll because it is too shy or too upset to talk for itself but this approach raises a problem. As the bonds between the children and the Doll deepen, would the Doll continue to be shy? An alternative might be to say to the children that we are going to pretend that the Doll is a child like them. To ensure that we establish that it really is a Doll we could ask them questions like:

- Is the Doll really alive?

- Can it breathe?

- Can it eat?

- Can it laugh and cry?

We could then suggest that they know and we know that it is a Doll and that it can't really talk but we are going to pretend that it can. It will 'talk' to us and we will tell them what it says. Passing the Doll around the circle at the beginning and/or the end of the session gives the children a chance for a quick greeting and a hug – it may be necessary to warn children that the Doll doesn't like children to pull its hair or undress it.

The capacity to wait and listen to someone else talking is essential to successfully achieving the goals associated with the Persona Doll storytelling process. To start with, the stories need to be short and simple because some children find it difficult to listen to a story that lasts longer than about five minutes and find it almost impossible to have to listen to each other after that. But as their concentration spans develop it should be possible to lengthen the stories and build up to more complicated ones. Over time the children will get to know a good many things about each of the Dolls, remember what happened to each one in the stories and be able to talk about how they and the Dolls felt.

When children meet the Doll for the first time the goal is to help them get to know it and become friends. With a Doll on our lap and in a relaxed and conversational tone of voice, we tell them some of the more important and interesting details about its persona – about its family and cultural background, where it lives and some of its favourite things. Throughout the session the children are encouraged to participate actively.

Introducing a Doll the children have met before involves choosing the goal – why the Doll is telling this particular story and what we hope the children will learn. We arouse everyone's interest by asking open-ended questions and by adding a few more details about the Doll's persona to deepen the bonds being developed between the children and the Doll. It is a good idea to begin by refreshing their memories about the Doll's life and personality, especially the features that relate to the story the Doll is about to tell them. They could be asked what they remember about its previous stories and how these stories made them feel.

Having told the children the story the Doll has come to tell them, we maximise their input. We might ask how they think the Doll feels about what has happened to it. This could be the goal and focus of the story so it is important to consider the emotions we want the story to evoke. By examining the feelings of the Doll the children can understand its motivation i.e. why it behaved/thought as it did.

However, a word of warning. Try not to introduce details that the children will need/want to discuss. For example, if we intend telling a story about a child who is being bullied and in the introduction say that the mother of the Doll we are using has just had a new baby, the children are likely to focus on this fact for the rest of the session. Bullying will need to be the theme of another story at another time!

Children can learn positive attitudes through empathising with the stories Dolls with disabilities tell them. But if they have never been in close contact with adults or children with disabilities, they may be frightened, anxious and upset when a child with a disability comes to the setting. Their knowledge, misinformation, prejudices and fears about disabilities are often revealed through the questions they ask, and we can respond with accurate information. One of the practitioners in a Children's Centre realised that the reason why some of the children didn't want to include Lesley, the only child who used a wheelchair, in their games was that they were worried and fearful. She told a story about a Doll called Anna. This enabled them to talk about their feelings and to recognize that Anna was like them in many ways but that she was also different from them – she was a wheelchair user. The children were able to express their feelings and ask questions in a safe and supportive environment.

According to Trisha Whitney (1999:4-5), the learning experience gained from having been involved in Persona Doll storytelling sessions will influence children's thinking and behaviour when they go to another setting. These two examples illustrate the impact the sessions can have.

> One young boy came home and asked, 'Why do they think boys are better than girls in my new school? In my old school we never thought that.'

> A European-American child came home from school and told her mother that she needed her hair done in many small braids. When her mother asked her about the reason for this urgent need, she replied, 'There's only one African-American girl in my class. The other kids tease her about her braids. I want braids too, so she won't be the only one.' This child wore her braids with pride, and showed the other children that it is possible to stand up against bias.

The Dolls and their stories provide us with a powerful tool but one that needs to be thoughtfully and wisely used. In the middle of a story, children may divulge emotionally-charged information, perhaps for the first time, and which possibly has nothing to do with the issue being raised in the story. If we inadvertently 'open a can of worms' in this way, our response will depend on the situation and the personality of the child, but as a general rule, it is best to acknowledge what has been said as briefly and calmly as possible and, if appropriate, continue with the story. Further steps will depend on the situation, the relationship with the family and advice from other practitioners. The question of confidentiality then arises. We are not therapists and it is important to refer children with severe emotional difficulties to those who can help them. Advice is available from the Child Psychotherapy Trust which has a 24 hour telephone helpline: 020 7485 5510 and a website helpline@cpth.fsnet.co.uk for people who work with children and families. It is not a good idea for us to use persona dolls to counsel children from abused backgrounds – that is a job for trained professionals.

After the storytelling session

In order to help us build a collection of appropriate and enjoyable stories, to improve our technique, to keep track of any issues arising that need to be incorporated into other stories and to maximise the children's input and learning, Whitney (1999:201) recommends that we evaluate each storytelling session.

We could spend time thinking about and evaluating whether it went according to plan, how the children responded, whether anything unexpected happened, whether it lived up to our expectations and what we might have said or done to heighten the impact. If the children seemed insufficiently engaged, we may decide to change or shorten the story or abandon it altogether. Thinking about how each child reacted can help us review our responses. Did we encourage the quiet children sufficiently? Did we pay more attention to some children's contributions than to others'?

Sessions could also be evaluated by colleagues or parents with whom we feel comfortable. Sitting in on sessions and later commenting on the presentation of the Doll, how the scene was set, the way the discussion was facilitated and how the children responded could be most helpful. The more often this is done, the less distracted we and the children would be by the evaluator's presence.

Even more helpful could be camcording sessions. Seeing ourselves telling the story is likely to be a learning experience! When Whitney (1999:201) records, she arranges the children in a horseshoe and she sits in the centre. The camcorder is set up at the opening of the horseshoe so that she and most of the children are in focus. It's a good idea to make recordings often so that the children become so used to the camera that they forget about it and so do we. We can choose whether we want to view the video in our own time and in private or whether to share it with colleagues so everyone can comment and learn from it. We can observe individual children's reactions, notice what we picked up on and what we missed, monitor our words and phrases for bias, check that we allowed children the time they needed to contribute and that we treated each child with equal concern.

When we successfully facilitate Persona Doll storytelling sessions we support and develop children's learning. We provide opportunities for them to extend and consolidate their knowledge and skills; to share ideas, experiences and feelings; expand their vocabularies and develop their ability to use language; explore, experiment and be creative. We build on their understanding of what is fair and unfair and we boost their confidence and self-esteem. No small achievement!

People will forget what you said ...

People will forget what you did ...

But people will never forget how you made them feel.

Source unknown.

5

Stories to tell

As the title suggests, this chapter includes a variety of stories to give practitioners and students ideas on which to build and develop their own stories.

The stories practitioners tell are generally based on what happens to the children while they are in the setting and on experiences reported by parents or the children themselves. Some of these may be similar to those described in the stories which follow. The stories are not intended to be recipes but rather to spark ideas and clarify the procedures and strategies outlined in the rest of the book.

Stories that deal with difficult situations experienced by the Dolls will probably arouse children's sympathy and empathy. These are the stories they are most likely to remember. But they need to be told stories about happy experiences as well as sad ones and encouraged to talk about their positive and negative emotions. Hearing many Persona Doll stories enables them to appreciate that it helps to tell somebody about their problems and that doing so often make things better. They might also come to the conclusion that some problems can't be solved.

This example about a Doll called Mei Lin, cited by Whitney (1999: 68), illustrates the structure of the storytelling process:

> Mei Lin cried and kicked and said she wouldn't go to the dentist, even though one of her teeth was hurting very badly. She was afraid the dentist would stick her with a long needle and then cut her tooth out with a knife!

during the feelings stage of this story the children identify Mei Lin's feelings of fear, worry and upset and during the discussion stage they tell her about their own experiences at the dentist. The adult reassures them that the dentist is careful and never cuts people. The resolution stage recounts the visit to the dentist and how afterwards her tooth didn't hurt Mei Lin anymore.

Most of our Persona Doll collection should reflect the children in the setting and their stories based on the children's experiences, attitudes and feelings. Children are often anxious about what will happen when they start school. How will the other children react to them? This story could be told to a group who are going to 'big school' and who may be worried about how their new peers will respond to them. They have met the Doll on many previous occasions.

After re-introducing George, the practitioner could begin telling his story.

George is worried.

Do you know what feeling worried means?

Have you ever felt worried?

What were you worried about?

What helped you to stop worrying?

Well, george is worried because he has got lots of freckles on his nose and on his cheeks.

Can you see them?

(The Doll could be passed around at this point)

He's worried that when he goes to his new school the children will laugh at his freckles and won't want to play with him.

How do you think that would make him feel?

But do you think the children will tease George about his freckles?

Have you ever been teased?

What did you do?

If he is teased about his freckles, what do you think George should do?

Some children find separating from a parent difficult. A story about a Persona Doll in a similar situation can help children deal with their own strong feelings. Having introduced a Persona Doll called Steven, the scene is set:

Steven says he didn't want his mum to leave him at the centre this morning. He was very upset and held her hand tightly. When she told him that she had to go, he clung on to her leg. he cried and cried when she left and he still feels like crying.

Steven would like to know if any of you have ever felt like this?

What made you feel better?

How can we help Steven?

Can you think of things he can do until his mum comes to fetch him?

How do you think Steven will feel when his mum comes?

How do you feel when it is time to go home?

Some of the children's parents may be divorced and the children may live most of the time with their mothers and stay with their fathers on weekends and holidays. An example of a situation familiar to some children but strange to others is incorporated into this story. They know Ann because the Doll had visited them several times, so once their memories have been jolted by asking questions and capturing their interest, the story can begin.

Ann wants to tell you about her little duck. She says that it is the fluffiest, cuddliest, yellow duck in the whole world. It's not a real duck but Anne pretends it is. She calls it 'Quack'.

Who do you think watches Ann when she has a bath?

Quack.

When Ann goes to sleep, who do you think sleeps in her bed?

Quack.

Who sits on the table while Ann has breakfast?

Quack.

Who watches TV with her?

Quack.

Ann wants to know if you have a favourite toy?

Ann would like to know if any of you live in a flat?

Ann would like to know if any of you live in a house?

Ann's friend Jake lives in a flat and her friend Rebecca lives in a house.

Ann is lucky. She lives in a flat and a house! Most of the time she lives with her Mum in their flat but she often stays with her Dad in his house.

Who do you think goes with her when she goes to her Dad's house?

You're right – Quack.

Who do you think watches Ann when she has a bath at her Dad's house?

Quack.

When Ann goes to sleep at her Dad's house, who do you think sleeps in her bed?

Quack.

The session can be brought to a close by encouraging the children to talk about their homes. Whether or not there are Gypsy/Traveller children in the setting, the practitioner should ensure that trailers are included and be sensitive to the fact that any recently arrived refugee children in the group may still be very upset at having had to leave their homes.

When drawing on actual incidents, whether in the group or at home, adapt the situation so that it does not exactly mirror the one a child is going through and, to avoid the child being recognised by the other children, switch the Doll's gender, ethnic group, or family background. Think beforehand about any children who are likely to be particularly affected by the story and constantly observe their reactions during the storytelling so they can be offered support if they seem uncomfortable.

Having learnt to identify emotions, the next step for the children involves discussing the situation and suggesting solutions. This might take the form of thinking about why the doll acted in that particular way, or practising putting themselves in the doll's shoes, or suggesting multiple solutions and choosing the best ones for all the characters in the story. The task of the storyteller is to reflect back what the children are saying, ask leading questions and pick up on contributions by the children most affected by the situation being discussed.

By observing and listening closely, practitioners can pick up on any superior attitudes expressed by children and then use the conversation to spark a story. One classroom assistant did this in an infant class. She overheard two children who were friends talking and felt that the superior attitude expressed by the one child needed to be countered, and support offered to her companion.

The first child had said in an incredulous and superior tone: "You mean you walk to school and to swimming and to the shops? Why? Haven't you got a car? We've got two cars. My dad's is blue and my mum's is red."

At circle time, a Doll called Fred told them his story.

Fred says he loves going for walks, especially with his Dad.

I like going for walks. Do you?

Last week they went for a picnic. They walked to the bus stop, chatting all the way. When the bus came they sat upstairs. Fred loved that. He says there was so much to see and to talk about.

He wonders if you often go on the bus like he does?

When they got to the park, Fred played on the swings. He was soon starving hungry. Luckily his Dad had brought Fred's favourite sandwiches.

Can you guess what they were?

Do you like sandwiches? What do you like on your sandwiches?

When everything was eaten up, Fred and his Dad went for a lovely long walk in the wood. When they got back it was time to go home.

They had to wait quite a long time for the bus. Fred didn't mind. He liked watching the people. Do you know what Fred told me? He said his Dad thinks that cars are noisy and smelly and they give him a headache. He thinks there should just be buses and trains.

Fred would like to know what you think.

Tackling Discrimination

By creating stories around discriminatory incidents occurring in the setting, we can encourage children to think critically and not stereo-typically. To participate in these storytelling sessions children need to have words such as fair, unfair, bias, respect, untrue in their voca-bulary and to understand their meaning. If we introduce these words into the stories and discussions, the children will be encouraged to use them and might eventually be able to evaluate certain events, ex-periences and feelings in their own lives. Their vocabulary should also include words that equip them to express how hurt and angry they feel when they are called names or teased and enable other children to express their sympathy and support. To heighten their awareness that discriminatory behaviour hurts, children need stories that help them feel what the Doll is feeling and to think deeply about issues. Discriminatory incidents could be followed up in later stories by showing how the children's suggestions helped the Doll deal with a similar situation or how a story changed the perpetrator's attitude and behaviour.

By listening carefully to what children say to each other throughout the day we can find out whether any of them are being physically abused, teased, threatened, or called hurtful names because of the colour of their skin, their physical features, their religion, the language(s) they speak, their abilities or the kind of family they live in.

A teacher in a nursery school in a middle class suburb of London overheard one little boy Christopher shouting at one of the few Black children in the group: 'Rachid go away. You can't play with us . My gran and me don't like brown people.'

Kylie and Geoffrey, who were playing nearby, immediately invited Rachid to join their game. At circle time the teacher told a Persona Doll story based on this incident. To ensure that it did not exactly mirror the situation, and to avoid the children being recognised she changed the setting, the circumstances and the gender of the main character but used a black doll. While she told the story she constantly observed Christopher and Rachid in case they needed her support and highlighted the positive responses of Kylie and Geoffrey.

> With the children expressing their delight at seeing Emily, one of the Persona Dolls sitting on the practitioner's lap, the storytelling session began. The Doll was passed around the circle. From the way each child greeted it, the teacher could see the extent to which they had bonded and how much they cared about it. From their animated responses to her questions it was obvious that the previous story had made an

impression, that they empathised with emily and wanted to hear her story.

Emily was having a really lovely time in the park on Sunday with her friends Lee, Alice and Jack. Emily wants to know what you like doing when you go to the park.

Well, Emily and her friends were having fun when some big children came along and asked Lee, Alice and Jack if they wanted to join in their game.

'Sure!' they replied.

Emily wanted to play but they said she was too small and small people were stupid so they didn't want her in their game. Off they ran leaving Emily all alone.

At this point the teacher maximised the children's input by asking questions like:

'What do you think Emily was feeling when the children said she couldn't play with them?'

'Do you sometimes feel like that?'

'Do you think small people are stupid?'

The children were eager to help Emily, particularly because they considered she had been unfairly treated. They enjoyed offering her their advice and talking about their own experiences and actions. They were further stimulated by being asked appropriate questions like:

Emily was the smallest. She might have spoilt their game. Do you think they were right not to want her to play?

Were they being fair?

If you saw what happened to Emily what would you have done?

If it happened again what do you think Emily should do?

The teacher brought the story to an appropriate conclusion by selecting contributions that most closely matched the goal of the story i.e. to highlight the pain of exclusion and the pleasure of being included. She particularly picked up on the contributions of Rachid and Christopher, as it was his negative remark to Rachid about brown people that had triggered the story. She stressed the intervention of the four children that mirrored Kylie's and Geoffrey's sensitive response to Rachid. She hoped that thinking about how Emily was treated might have helped Christopher gain insight into his own prejudiced attitude. She also expanded their vocabulary of 'feeling' words.

Like all children, those with disabilities are able to relate to and draw strength from stories about situations and experiences similar to their own. Children with learning difficulties may experience teasing and be excluded from play. The following story could be told to try and change the situation by giving the other children some insight into their own behaviour and attitude.

I wonder if you remember who this is? That's right, it is Abigail. Last time she came to visit us, she was very happy. Who can remember what made her so happy? You have got good memories. She went on a train for the first time in her life. But today Abigail is not at all happy. The problem is that the children at her nursery school have started calling her dozy Abigail and silly Abigail.

How do you think that makes Abigail feel?

Her teacher told them that it wasn't nice to say things like that and that they must play nicely with her.

So they let Abigail join in their game but it was no good. They said she didn't play properly and they shouted at her and they called her Slowcoach, Slowcoach.

She didn't like that! So she walked away. She stood all by herself and watched the children playing.

How do you think Abigail felt?

She wants to know what you would have done if you saw what happened?

The children will probably be eager to help Abigail because her classmates were being horrible to her.

The next story was told in response to a child remarking to another, 'Why don't you answer me? Are you deaf or something?' The fact that the teacher was able to sign heightened the children's involvement in the story and their ability to empathise.

You haven't met Jack before. He is five years old. Lots of you are five. Jack's glad so many of you are the same age as he is. He lives in a flat. He wants to know if some of you also live in a flat?

Nearly everybody.

Jack has a big sister and a baby brother just like lots of you. But there is something about Jack that is different from all of you and he wants me to tell you what it is. He doesn't hear sounds as clearly as you do. When people talk to him he doesn't hear what they are saying, because he is deaf.

But Jack has got his own way of talking. He makes words with his hands and fingers in a special way. When other people make words with their hands and fingers in the same special way then Jack can understand what they are saying. They are talking in sign language. It is also called signing.

Don't you think Jack is very clever to be able to talk in this very special way?

Would you like to be able to talk in this special way? I could teach you, then we will all be able to sign to Jack and he will be able to sign back to us. Jack says that would be great.

Jack told me that he had a lovely surprise yesterday. His gran came to his house with a big box. Can you guess what was inside the box?

No, it wasn't lego though he would have liked that.

He does love reading but it wasn't a book.

No, it wasn't a bicycle.

Should I tell you what it was?

It was a little black and white puppy called Spot!

Jack loves Spot and he says Spot loves him. Jack is worried in case Spot is missing him. So he wants to go home now but he will come and visit us again soon.

Cross-cultural respect and understanding can be built by introducing Dolls that do not reflect the children in the group. This is particularly important where the children are all from the same ethnic or cultural group and speak the dominant language. For example, in a setting in which there are no Turkish children a Doll with a Turkish background could be introduced. It would be the first time the children are meeting Hatice although they have met and heard stories about other Persona Dolls.

Would you like to meet Hatice? She is four years old. She lives with her Mum and Dad and her three brothers in a flat. She's very clever because she can speak Turkish and English. Hatice has got a Grandma and a Grandpa. They talk to her in Turkish.

Hatice wants to know if you've got a Grandma and a Grandpa?

She calls her Grandma and Grandpa, 'Babaanne'.

She wants to know if you've got a special name for your Grandma and Grandpa?

Babaanne live in a house near to Hatice's flat. Hatice loves going to visit them.

They always have her favourite chocolate waiting for her.

Can you guess what it is?

If it's not raining or too freezing cold Hatice plays in the garden because she hasn't got a garden at her flat. But she also likes watching TV with her Babaanne. They let her choose any programme she wants to watch. Then they all eat little cakes called Baklava. Hatice loves them because they've got nuts and honey inside them! Babaanne drinks coffee in little cups and Hatice has milk in her own special cup.

Hatice has some exciting news to tell you. She's got another Grandpa and he's coming to visit Hatice. He lives far far away in a country called Turkey. Hatice has never ever seen him. But she knows what he looks like because she has a photo of him on a table in her bedroom. She's spoken to him on the phone so she knows what his voice sounds like. She calls him, 'Annenanne'.

Hatice needs your advice. She is going to the airport to meet Anneanne and she would like to give him a present but she can't think what to make. Can you help her?

The children will probably offer suggestions and the story can be wrapped up by telling them that Hatice said they had given her so many ideas she was going to try and make all the presents they suggested for Anneanne.

During a story a child might express prejudice, stereotypical thinking or misinformation. We might be able to deal with it within the story through the Doll or it might be best to comment just briefly and continue with the story. We could take up the issue again in another story, perhaps one in which the Doll initially believes something that is incorrect and then learns the truth.

The following incident illustrates how children's comments during a story can highlight the need for an issue to be the subject of another one.

The children had been told a story about Rosie, one of the Persona Dolls, and what she wanted to be when she grew up. Afterwards they talked about what they would like to be. Julie, who uses a wheelchair, said she wanted to be a scientist like her Mum. Tony laughed and said, 'How can you do that? You can't even walk'.

The other children expressed their agreement.

Weaving this incident into a story about a boy doll who had a disability, the practitioner gave Tony and the other children correct information and hoped that this and the empathy that the story had elicited would encourage them to reflect on their prejudiced and hurtful response.

Problem-solving and thinking critically

Once they have learnt to identify emotions and to empathise, the next step is for the children to discuss the situation and propose solutions. It is at this point that children learn and practice problem-solving skills and suggest ways in which the Dolls can stand up for themselves and others. They are concerned about the Dolls and keen to offer advice, especially when the stories highlight situations or experiences that they consider unfair. If the children don't offer solutions, they can be prompted by our suggesting a few of our own.

Present simple and straightforward problems – the younger the children the simpler the problems. Show them that there are several ways to solve a problem, encourage them to think about why the Doll acted in a particular way, practise putting themselves in the Doll's shoes and suggest strategies for dealing with the problem. Having experience helping the Dolls to solve their problems can provide children with skills to solve their own problems and enable them to express their own pent-up feelings.

After questioning the children to ensure they remembered the Doll, Thandanani, the teacher told them about her problem.

Thandanani goes to swimming lessons every Monday afternoon. That's not the problem. She likes being in the water. She's not scared like she used to be. She can put her face right into the water. The problem is that her swimming teacher says her name is too hard to say so she calls her Narni. The children also call her Narni. Thandanani doesn't like to be called Narni because it isn't her real name. She loves her name and she thinks Narni sounds horrible. She's not Narni, she's Thandanani.

And another thing. There are other children in her swimming class who also have long names but the teacher calls them by their real names. She doesn't call Madeline, 'Line' or Annamaria, 'Ria'.

How do you think Thandanani feels when the teacher and the children call her Narni?

She wants to know if people say your name properly? How does it make you feel if they get it wrong?

Do people sometimes call you a name you don't like?

Can you help Thandanani? Is there anything she can do to get her teacher to call her Thandanani?

Problem-solving skills require an ability to think flexibly and critically, to visualise a range of realistic solutions, to describe the problems accurately and listen to everyone's concerns. These skills help children respond fairly and sympathetically in social situations and develop their ability to think critically. Our role is to create stories that have a range of possible solutions, ask leading questions, reflect back what the children are saying and pick up particularly on the contributions of those who are affected by the situation being discussed.

Refugee children, especially those who have recently arrived in the UK, are vulnerable to hurtful comments directed at them. This story for school-aged children is woven around a Persona Doll called Khan Tho, who is not a refugee, to ensure that the refugee children are not targeted. The children have met Khan Tho before so a few minutes would need to be spent questioning them to check on what they remember about her and about the stories that have been told about her.

Do you know where Khan Tho lives? You're right. She lives in a flat round the corner from our nursery school. She has lived there all her life – ever since she was a teeny tiny baby. But Khan Tho told me that her Mum and Dad haven't always lived in the flat. Long before Khan Tho was born her Mum and Dad lived in a country called Vietnam. She wonders if any of your family used to live in another country.

Vietnam is very very far away from London. Can you guess how they came all the way from Vietnam to London?

You've all suggested that they came in an aeroplane. That would have been a good way to come but it costs a lot of money. They had to come on a small boat. It took a very long time.

Khan Tho has never been to Vietnam. Her Mum and Dad tell her lots of stories about when they lived there. Khan Tho's Gran and Grandpa still live in Vietnam and Khan Tho would love to go and visit them. Her Mum and Dad told her that they will all go as soon as they have enough money.

Khan Tho is usually a happy girl but yesterday something happened that really upset her. It was milk and fruit time at her nursery school and she wanted to sit next to Alice. But Alice said she didn't want to sit next to Khan Tho because she has funny brown eyes.

Let's look at Khan Tho's eyes. I think they're beautiful. Alice was wrong. Khan Tho's eyes are not funny. They are just a different shape from Alice's eyes. Let's look at each others eyes. Are they all the same shape and colour?

Are our noses all the same shape?

How do you think Khan Tho felt when Alice said she didn't want to sit next to her?

What would you have done if you were there?

Has anybody ever been unkind like that to you?

Khan Tho says she feels better because she can see that we think being nasty to people about the way they look is unkind and unfair. She says we're right. We shouldn't make fun of other children and they shouldn't make fun of us.

The children can be helped to understand that name-calling, excluding others from play and hurting them is not fair. By providing them with information, promoting empathy, encouraging them to observe each other carefully, they can notice and value the similarities and differences between them. The refugee children will need to be empowered gradually to confront any prejudiced attitudes and behaviour they're facing, and ideally, the other children will support them.

Merging questions into the stories encourages children to identify with the Dolls, see the injustice of situations and consider solutions. This helps them to think creatively and critically about problems in their own lives. When we tell a new story we can reinforce messages from other happy and sad stories by reminding the children about previous incidents involving that particular Doll.

Persona Doll stories address issues as they arise and before they surface as well as those we believe children should have opportunities to think about. This story could raise the awareness of a group of 6 year old monolingual children.

Minka would like to tell you what happened to her yesterday. She and her friend were having fun in the park. They had made a little house for themselves under a big tree. While they were pretending to cook their lunch two big boys came over and shouted in loud frightening voices.

Why don't you talk properly? Why don't you speak English?

In a quiet little voice Minka told them she can speak English but she likes speaking Cantonese.

Do you know what the boys shouted back?

We can talk funny too. Listen. Hoi moi me moi. Your language is stupid and you're stupid.

Minka started to cry and so did her friend. They didn't like it when the boys pretended to be speaking Cantonese. They were glad when the boys walked away.

Minka wants to know if anyone has ever told you that you're stupid?

How did you feel?

What do you think she should do if she and her friend meet those boys again?

Minka says she likes speaking Cantonese to her friends. She doesn't think it's fair that she should speak English if she doesn't feel like it. Do you think it's fair?

She wants to know if we would like to learn some Cantonese words?

She's so glad we do. She says she'll teach us how to say hello next time she comes to visit us. She might even teach us to sing a song in Cantonese!

Incidents like the following could be woven into a Persona Doll story to give children opportunities to talk about how they feel when adults lay down the rules.

As a six-year-old boy told me, 'I like painting best but you can only paint at choosing time. Miss says only one person at a time, no paint on the floor, don't mix the paints, one picture each so every one gets a turn and only if you've finished all your work. I don't think that's fair.' Duffy (1998)

Being involved in problem solving can help children to think critically and realise that sometimes the things they have been told are not true.

> Ben wants to know if you can help him. There's something he doesn't understand. He asked his mum why his friend John has brown skin. She said it was because he came from a very hot country and got burnt by the sun. But John told Ben that he's never been to a very hot country. His Mum and Dad haven't either.
>
> Why do you think John has brown skin?

The children could be told that melanin makes skin dark or light. If they have a lot of melanin their skin will be dark and if they have a little, their skin will be light. How much melanin they have depends on how much their mum's and dad's have.

When using more than one Doll in a story, think about the relationship between them and what the children might learn from each one. You could introduce two Dolls that the children have already met to tell their own version of the same story – presenting two points of view. Or you could use three Dolls and have two involved in a discriminatory incident that is witnessed by the third Doll. The problem the children have to solve is what the third doll should do. More than one Doll can be used to illustrate a conflict situation in which the Dolls change their minds as a result of the discussion, but children also need to see that the Dolls might continue to disagree – not all conflicts and problems are soluble.

Wrapping up a story

The ending of a story, like the introduction, needs to be kept short and simple – about six or seven sentences to bring it to an appropriate, but not necessarily perfect, conclusion. Children enjoy giving advice and suggestions to the dolls and talking about their own experiences and actions. Include their contributions, particularly those most closely matching the goal of the story – what you hoped the children would learn.

Letting the Dolls thank the children for caring about them and helping them to solve their problems can make the children feel good about themselves and about being part of the group. Wrapping up the story involves telling the children what the doll decided to do and weaving in their contributions.

> Robert is really pleased that he came to visit you today. He says you are good friends to care about him and help him feel less worried. He says that Liz had a good idea. He's going to ask his mum to give him a photo of his dad and he will keep it in his special drawer. He can look at it when he has that funny feeling in his tummy. He thinks Aziz is right. If he does lots of things while he's at playgroup then he won't miss his dad so much. As soon as he comes with his mum in the morning he says he's going to play with the sand and then with the water. He likes Tom's idea too. He will do all the things that make him happy.

Even though Persona Doll stories raise issues in a non-threatening way, children often need reassurance – they care about the Dolls and need to know that they are alright at the end of the story. So even if the main goal was not about dealing with strong emotions, include one or two sentences describing how the Doll(s) successfully handle their feelings.

A story to illustrate this learning process:

> David tells the children that he really really wants to be friends with Yasmin, but she doesn't want to be friends with him. Yesterday she was playing with Emily and Wendy. He asked if he could play with them. Yasmin said he couldn't because he's a boy and she only plays with girls.

> The children are asked to describe David's feelings – he was sad, upset and disappointed. They are likely to feel sorry for him and want to help. They could talk about times when children hadn't wanted to play with them and how that had made them feel.

When the children are asked why they thought Yasmin didn't want to play with boys, they offered a number of reasons and suggested possible solutions. After these had been evaluated by the children, the teacher selected and ended the story by feeding back the appropriate responses such as, 'David decided that you were right. If Yasmin doesn't want to play with him, he will find someone else to play with.'

Given time, respect and a supportive environment, older children can be encouraged to use the Dolls to tell their own stories. They might, for example, share what happened the night before when the lights went out and nobody could remember where the candles were, or about how their mum reacted when the puppy piddled on the carpet, or about what happened when 'somebody' put the plug in the sink and left the tap running. Their stories will reflect diverse family values and lifestyles. The way in which we listen to these stories will send powerful messages about our attitudes. If we respond by, for instance, raising eyebrows or asking questions in disbelief, we will probably silence them.

Some scenarios

The stories we create need to evolve out of the day to day experiences and situations in the group. But as some are common to many early years settings, these suggestions might help you get started.

There are no other Black children in Max's class. When the children go out to play they say they don't want to play with him. Sometimes they hit him and punch him. Sometimes they call him names. It makes him feel very miserable. He doesn't know what to do. He wonders if you can help him.

Marie is feeling very happy. Her teacher says she can look after Hazel, who will be coming to school for the first time tomorrow. Marie remembers how worried she was on her first day and how glad she was that Michael looked after her. Hazel can't see very well. What do you think Marie should do to help her?

William wants to know if you think it's alright for boys to cry. His mum thinks it's OK and so does his Gran. But yesterday he cried when he fell down and hurt himself really badly. His cousins called him a cry-baby and told him big boys don't cry.

Adam is going to his friend Clara's party. She's going to be 5. He wonders what he should give her for a present. Have you got any ideas?

John says he wishes children would stop teasing him because he lives in a trailer. He thinks living in a trailer is fun and he's glad he doesn't live in a house. But he really doesn't like it when children are horrible to him. He thinks it isn't fair. What should he do?

Alice and Tina are twins. Alice loves climbing trees and riding her bike as fast as she can. Tina always wants to play dolls and tea parties. Alice thinks that's boring. Tina thinks climbing trees and riding bikes is very boring. They want to know if you can think of games they could play together?

Frank is excited. He's going to do something he's never done before. His mum is taking him to choose some glasses so he'll be able to see properly. He's a bit worried though because his big sister told him he'll be teased and called 'four eyes'.

Jamie and his friend Tony have been arguing. Jamie says that children can't have two mothers and Tony says they can. Who is right?

Stories woven around the Dolls encourage young children to develop empathy and respect for people different from themselves. The hope is that when they grow up they won't judge others by the colour of their skin, their physical features, their disabilities, their gender or their sexual orientation.

6

Including parents

This chapter focuses on why parents need to feel included in the settings their children attend and, more specifically, on the need to consult and involve them when Persona Dolls are selected and their personas created. Also discussed is the possibility of the Dolls going home with children and what parents will need to do.

We know that parents are the most important people in their children's lives and their first teachers. Building partnerships with parents is required by the 1989 Children Act and the Guidance and Regulations Vol 2 as well as by the DfEE's Draft Revised Code of Practice on the Identification and Assessment of Pupils with Special Educational Needs (2000). All local authorities need to make arrangements for parent partnership services. The aim is to ensure that parents have access to information and support to enable them to make informed and appropriate decisions in relation to their children's education. If parents feel from the outset that they are supported, informed and respected as equal partners in decision-making, some of the extra pressure of caring for a child with special needs can be eased.

Building collaborative relationships between parents and practitioners is also a key process involved in implementing anti-discriminatory practice. The aim is to inform and empower parents by acknowledging their qualities and skills and by giving them time and opportunities to voice their concerns. We learn a great deal from parents about their children and we offer them our expertise and experience to draw on. How they respond to us depends largely on the way we communicate with them.

For example:

Are discussions about their children collaborative or based on the idea that as professionals we know best?

Is our relationship with certain parents influenced by how they are labelled?

Do we perceive assertive parents as aggressive, and respond accordingly?

A first step towards establishing positive working relationships is getting to know each parent individually. When we take on board their different perceptions, aspirations, experiences and personalities as well as the diverse ways in which they are raising their children, we will probably conclude that there is no single 'best' way to bring up children. We are less likely to make inaccurate assumptions and judgements if we appreciate that although the lifestyles of children from the same cultural group will have much in common, each family practises its culture and raises their children in its own way. Parents can help us recognise also the many forms of physical and mental disability, and the degree to which they can vary.

The second step is to listen and respond to parents' wishes so that together we can create a collaborative, constructive, equitable and non-threatening working environment in which everyone feels equally valued. If practitioners look for and acknowledge the qualities and skills parents have to offer, the parents will become more confident and involved. In a supportive environment like this practitioners and parents can be open and flexible, willing to consult and negotiate, learn from each other, share experiences, and respect and trust each other. In a two-way learning process effective and rewarding relationships can be built. Everyone receives positive affirmation for words and actions that express kindness, empathy and concern. Consequently, practitioners and parents benefit and conditions are created in which all children can blossom. But establishing and maintaining relationships is not always easy. It involves commitment, understanding, patience and a variety of negotiating skills. If conflict and misunderstandings do occur, they need to be openly discussed.

Parents under pressure

As educators we know that young children are profoundly influenced by their families and by the communities in which they live. To build collaborative relationships with parents we also need to understand the difficulties many of them face. This presents us with a challenge. Are we sufficiently empathetic to be able to provide the support, friendship and reassurance many parents seek?

We may not always appreciate how difficult and exhausting parenting can be. Many parents are struggling against enormous odds and doing the best they can given the inadequate resources and competing pressures they have to contend with. Many find themselves in a cycle of poverty and deprivation – as illustrated by this mother's comment:

> I wanted better for my kids. Instead it gets worse. My kids have never had a traditional Sunday dinner – if they get meat, it's corned beef or sausages... The Government has no idea what we are going through, that we struggle to better ourselves and we get pushed back. If those Government ministers could just come here and listen to us... Then I could tell them that my son has an iron deficiency because of his poor diet and that my daughter's asthma equipment was cut off with the electricity supply when I could not pay the bill. (Brown 1999:48)

Refugee parents come from different national, ethnic, cultural and linguistic backgrounds. They bring with them wide-ranging skills, qualifications and expertise, which frequently go unrecognised. Many are lonely and depressed women coping with their children without the support of their extended families. Black refugee adults and children are dealing not only with prejudice and the problems associated with being a refugee but also with the wider aspect of prejudice: racism. We need to be especially sensitive when asking refugee parents for background information about their children. Many have painful memories of interrogation in their own countries and so find trusting people difficult, particularly if they have been tortured. Finding out about the political situation in the countries from which families have fled and trying to understand the experiences they have been through and the difficulties involved in settling into a strange, often hostile, environment can be helpful.

Naomi Richman (1998:45) reports, '*An Iraqi man who had been tortured and whose wife had been killed was so suspicious that he would not agree to having an Iraqi interpreter even though his English was very limited.*'

Parents' own school experiences often influence their attitudes. Those who had a successful school career are likely to welcome the opportunity to build collaborative relationships with us but those whose experiences were unhappy might be less willing to do so or might feel they have nothing to offer.

Gypsy/Traveller mothers are generally worried that their children will be teased, called names and physically abused and may resist being separated from them. They are often scandalised at the way mothers in the settled community arrange for their children to be cared for by non-family members. According to Rutter (2001), this is also alien to certain refugee groups.

Parents who in their home countries were not expected to participate in their children's setting may be surprised and confused when asked to do so. Richman (1998:62) explains that Turkish parents often tell the teacher when they bring their child to school, '*Here is my child, the flesh is yours, but the bones are mine.*' On the other hand parents may need reassurance that we do not allow children to hurt each other verbally or physically.

Parents who are gay or lesbian are likely to be painfully aware of the prejudice and hostility that characterises homophobia. They have the right to keep their sexual orientation private and may decide to do so. They may be worried about the repercussions on their children or feel that the practitioners will disapprove and talk about them behind their backs. Parents may have heterosexual and lesbian/gay relationships at different times in their lives. Many lesbian mothers have had children while in previous heterosexual or homosexual relationships and may have encountered professionals who think that lesbian mothers are not fit to care for their children. When the custody of children is contested, the ability of a heterosexual mother is seldom questioned but a lesbian mother is likely to be closely examined.

To ensure that we respond appropriately to children whose cultural background is different from our own, we need to find out about and pay attention to the cultural patterns of care and learning styles in their homes. Paley (1995:18: 52: 130) cites the reasons why this needs to be a regular part of our work with young children, as suggested by two Black parents and a Native American mother:

> ... Black children should have a deep grounding in their own sense of self before the age of five or six. They must know early on that their history and culture have as much merit as anyone else's. Then they can go into any environment and not shut down.

> ... there is a cultural heritage that would not be present in the school community or in the communication patterns of teachers. Here is a Black child who loves his parents. But he goes to a school where so much of who his parents are means very little... If I see that teachers reach out to me and my family and want to include us, then I would choose that school.

> ... [My] children's school gave them no 'safe passage'. What we teach at home is not respected or even known in school... Among our people, for example, it is considered improper to make oneself appear smarter than others. But the teachers, who are mostly white, mistake our children's reticence for dullness or rebelliousness, The children feel ashamed. This is wrong.

During Persona Doll storytelling sessions we encourage children to talk about their family practices and so provide opportunities for practitioners and children to learn about a range of experiences. The cultures of all the children and their families are supported and respected and are reflected in other parts of the daily programme and in the resources we provide.

Parents and the Dolls

Before introducing the Dolls we need to involve parents, explain the reasons why we think their children could benefit, what we aim to do, and then decide together how these aims could best be achieved. Perhaps a special meeting could be arranged which is both an information-giving session and a demonstration of telling a Persona

Doll story. The subject might cover, for example, bullying, or seek to support parents who might be having difficulty acknowledging their child's impairment. Involving parents can ensure that appropriate Dolls are selected and accurate personas and stories created.

In a letter (translated if necessary) or in conversation we could say something on the lines suggested by Whitney (1999:204):

> We would like to create a persona for a doll that accurately represents a child from your culture (or a child with a particular disability). We will get to know the Doll and at the same time get to know about its culture (or disability). Would you be willing to help us? We will not make the Doll's persona exactly like your child or your family, of course, but information about your family will help us choose characteristics for the Doll and its family and themes for the stories.

This letter from the practitioners at a Kindergarten in Australia to parents gave information about the Dolls and explained that they hoped the stories would help children to think critically about what is fair and unfair and to act if they witnessed unfairness. As the Dolls would be visiting the children's homes, the letter included the rules that had been devised around the Dolls. Here are some of them:

- At Kindergarten the dolls are not to be left out as part of regular play. They must stay on the piano when not being used.

- They are called dolls and the children accept the stories as real but remember that they are 'only dolls'.

- The dolls can be borrowed overnight (Mon.-Wed.) with their bags of clothing and diary in which their life stories are written for parents to refer to.

- Parents are asked to record in the diary what the doll did while in their home (photos and drawings may be included).

- Any additions by practitioners to the dolls' life stories will have a coloured border. We encourage parents to read these segments to maintain consistency.

- Play with the dolls must be supervised – these are very special dolls.

- Please keep the diary out of the reach of children.

- Please return the dolls, the diary and the overnight bag promptly the next morning. (Jones and Mules 1997:42)

The Dolls become so 'real' to the children that their parents occasionally confuse the Dolls with the children in the setting, as this incident illustrates:

> A 4 year old excitedly informed his mother that his friend Melissa was going to spend Christmas with them. His distraught mother rushed up to one of the practitioners and apologetically explained that she was sorry but it was out of the question. Melissa couldn't stay with them. Her sister and her husband plus their three children were coming and there was no way that she could fit another child into the house. She was greatly relieved and amused to hear that Melissa was a Doll!

Following the visit, practitioners could share with the children the entry the parent had written in the Doll's diary and the children can talk about what happened when the Dolls visited them and how they felt. This exchange process can strengthen the bridge between children's homes and the setting, as this example from Australia illustrates:

> Ming, the persona doll that we've been using all year, has a back-pack, spare clothes, a teddy, a book, a toothbrush etc and a diary that all go with him when he goes to visit children and their families. Families write in the experiences Ming has when he visits (usually adding photos, drawings etc). This has provided a real insight for us into the children's lives at home, and a strong connection between these two parts of children's lives, home and Kindy (Kindergarten). Parents are particularly interested in the use of the dolls and the purpose of the dolls. One child announced to her mother that she'd like to be Chinese Australian too and another expressed concern as to whether Ming would eat mashed potato for dinner when he visited or whether they should cook noodles to make him feel at home – parents share these little stories with us and talk about the best way to respond and answer children's questions.

Sending the Dolls home with the children can benefit not only children but also their parents. By getting to know the Dolls, telling stories around them and adding to their diaries, parents are able to contribute actively to their children's learning. Those parents who lack self-esteem may feel especially gratified. A possible spin-off might be heightened parental involvement in other activities in the setting.

A Persona Doll table and a Persona Doll noticeboard could keep parents informed about the stories being told and could include the Dolls' visiting experiences if they go home with the children. It might be useful, particularly for those parents who can't come into the setting, to have a newsletter which keeps them in touch with what is happening to the Dolls. When the addition of new Dolls is being considered, parents could be encouraged to contribute their views and help with buying or making the Dolls.

The reaction of parents to the Dolls and their stories can vary considerably. Judy Dunn's research on relationships (1987:38) suggests that children whose mothers talk to them about feelings 'become particularly articulate about and interested in feeling states.' It seems reasonable to assume therefore that parents who encourage and develop their children's ability to empathise will respond to the Dolls and their stories with enthusiasm and commitment. They will probably be pleased to see how the Dolls build the children's capacity to put themselves in other people's shoes. When we start telling stories around equality issues, however, we might find that some parents are less co-operative and understanding. We could be confronted by parents who are upset and angry. Our knowledge about child development may be fine and our practice with the children 'spot-on', but in this situation we might not have the skills to respond to parents who express discriminatory attitudes and who might also be aggressive.

Derman-Sparks *et al* (1989) remind us that:

> ...our society gives people permission to use racism, sexism, or handicappism as outlets for frustration, anger, greed and fear. These facts do not make the bias OK but they help us to look at the whole

person and not just at the biased behaviour... Engage the parents in exploring their fears about what may happen to their child as a consequence of anti-bias education and in exploring your ideas about the benefits. Remember that this is a dialogue, not a monologue; make sure that parents have ample opportunity to express their views and that you are open to learning from their views as well as hoping they will learn from yours.

The goal is for everyone to express their feelings in a respectful way, listen to one another's point of view and negotiate a resolution of the conflict that both can accept. If either party feels threatened, they may react aggressively, refuse to consider alternatives, and the encounter could produce a hardening of attitudes instead of generating change. By learning to be assertive but not aggressive, listening carefully to parents' views, using legislation like the Children Act and the setting's equality policy we might win them over. They may realise that raising issues through the stories and discussing them fosters their children's personal, social, emotional and intellectual development and so helps them achieve the Early Learning Goals. However, if the parents have entrenched discriminatory beliefs, values and attitudes it may be impossible to change them.

That conflict situations can arise when parents object to the way the Dolls are used to address equality issues underlines the importance of there being an equality policy in the setting that is owned by parents and practitioners. All parents, and particularly those who are new to the setting, need time and many opportunities to discuss and comment on the policy. It is essential that they understand how the policy impacts on their children's learning and behaviour. Practitioners can hold discussions to explain that the setting operates on the equality principles enshrined in it and that these principles are not negotiable. Parents need to feel free to suggest changes to the policy but the equality principles must be held firm.

Developing, implementing and monitoring the policy requires the involvement of as many of the parents as possible. In the process people are likely to bond closer through the growth of shared understandings. In a constructive atmosphere everyone is more likely to feel able to question and express their opinions, to identify shared values, goals and strategies and to suggest ways to achieve them. Continuous evaluation and monitoring can identify the changes that need to be made and provide helpful insights into the way we work with and relate to colleagues and parents. All new practitioners need to be inducted into the terms of the policy and have opportunities to discuss its aims, objectives and the implications for their work, as well as their feelings and beliefs. 'Old' practitioners can be encouraged to involve new ones in the monitoring and evaluating process. Involvement enables everyone to feel that they 'own' the policy, that they have a vested interest in it.

Training with parents

Once we feel confident about telling Persona Doll stories to the children we might like to run a session with parents. The following programme was used with a small group of parents before Persona Dolls were introduced into the setting. They responded enthusiastically to the idea of using Dolls to combat discrimination and offered practical suggestions about how to involve parents. This programme would need to be adapted to meet local conditions.

After sharing three or four points about themselves, for example around their gender, ethnicity, family, favourite leisure activities, the parents and trainers considered some ground rules.

This was followed by the first task: Talk with the person sitting next to you about the sort of people you hope your children will be when they grow up and the sort of personalities you hope they will have.

During the feedback session a close correlation was noted between their aspirations and what we hope the children will gain from the Dolls and the stories.

Parents worked on the second task in groups of three: Among yourselves discuss how you know when someone likes or dislikes you. How you feel when you get the message that somebody likes you and when she/he dislikes you.

During the feedback, parents noted the crucial part non-verbal and verbal communication played and the feelings aroused.

The practitioner then talked about the reasons why Persona Dolls were to be introduced into the setting and the importance of selecting appropriate Dolls. How a Doll and its persona might be presented to the children was modelled. The parents were asked to respond as though they were the 'children'.

For task three, parents worked in small groups. Each group selected a Doll and developed a persona for it – its family and cultural background, where it lives, where it sleeps, the languages it speaks, the things it likes doing and those it doesn't, the things it can do and the things it finds difficult. They found it helpful to draw on their own children's personalities and preferences.

During feedback the parents shared the personas they had developed.

After the main features of Persona Doll stories were outlined and a storytelling session modelled, parents were once again invited to ask questions and comment.

They then brainstormed:

- their ideas for telling other parents about the Dolls and keeping them informed

- what they thought about the possibility of children having a Doll visit for the night

- their feelings about having to contribute to the Doll's diary.

The session was brought to a close.

Celebrating festivals with Persona Dolls

By incorporating parents' wishes into the anti-discriminatory curriculum we can offer festival activities that support what they learn at home. The Dolls can broaden children's general knowledge and correct misconceptions they may have about other people's festivals.

Persona Dolls provide us with a perfect tool because they can tell stories about how they celebrate festivals in their homes. Discussions can reveal the differences and similarities in the way families who share a religion practice it, and the fact that some families don't practice any religion. For example, Derman-Sparks (1989:93) suggests we tell a story about how a Jewish Doll's family celebrates Chanukah even if there are no Jewish children in the group. In another story the same Doll could tell a story about her friend who is also Jewish but whose family didn't celebrate it.

By celebrating social justice festivals such as Kwanzaa, Passover and Chanukah, children learn about how people's struggles in the past created a better life for themselves and others. Persona Doll stories created around these festivals can trigger discussions about people working for justice today. For example, a Black Persona Doll can be used to tell the children how its family celebrates Kwanzaa – a Swahili word meaning 'first fruits of the harvest. Kwanzaa was founded in the USA in 1966 by civil rights activist and academic Dr Maulana Ron Karenga to celebrate Black people's African heritage. She felt that Black Americans needed a festival to raise their consciousness of themselves, their history and the principles of unity, community and family that had helped their ancestors endure slavery and oppressions. It is a cultural rather than a religious festival. For seven days in December the virtues that strengthen family and community are honoured and practised. Children receive gifts that emphasise African culture, like musical instruments and books to celebrate the value of learning in African culture throughout its history.

Women's Day on the 8th of March offers children, practitioners and parents an opportunity to honour the women they know, as well as famous women. Except for the Doll telling a story about what it did on the day, the other Dolls sit on their own chairs in the circle, listening to the stories being told to the children.

In many settings Mother's Day and Father's Day cards and sometimes gifts are made with the children. When deciding whether or not to celebrate these events, we need to consider not only the diversity of families but to think about the individual families of the children. Some may have no money to buy a gift, others may not have a mother or father and others may have two mothers or two fathers. Approaches are needed that perhaps focus on the tasks family members do in and outside the home. Persona Dolls and their stories could provide information, trigger discussion and raise children's awareness of different family structures and practices. As Dau (1996:128) reminds us:

> The children in our early childhood services who come from homes where there is love and gentleness may be willing and enthusiastic to make cards for Father's Day or Mother's Day. If a child comes from a home where there is warfare and violence, how does this child feel when asked to celebrate either of these days? Children need choice about what they celebrate.

Persona Doll stories can encourage children to consider the mass marketing and commercialisation of festivals like Christmas, Halloween and Easter and to focus instead on giving, caring and sharing.

Parents and festivals

Festivals add spice to daily life by providing a break in the usual routine. They can also bring feelings of anticipation and excitement into the room. However, although discussions can give children accurate information about the meaning behind the symbols, songs, smells and festival artifacts, many of the concepts and symbols are too abstract and complex for young children to understand – especially for those who are newcomers to Britain.

Celebrating festivals like Diwali and Chinese New Year are fun and help children learn about a number of cultures. But they are unlikely to have much effect on their attitudes towards adults and children from these cultures especially if this is the only time that the particular culture is focused on. When festivals are presented in an anti-racist framework the misinformation, stereotypes and prejudices within the group are likely to be exposed and critical thinking encouraged. To ensure that the festivals we celebrate offer children accurate information and do not perpetuate stereotypes we need to consult with parents and other individuals in the community, and refer to books and cultural centres and libraries.

We need to think about why we celebrate particular festivals and how we celebrate them. In order to be able to reflect their home practices appropriately, we need to know which festivals the families celebrate, how they celebrate them and if and how they would like us to celebrate them. Not all parents will want us to celebrate their festivals. Some may feel that children should celebrate festivals within their own community and not outside it and others that festivals shouldn't be celebrated at all. Chat to parents and/or send them a questionnaire, translated if required. This one is based on Julie Bisson's (1997:43).

Sample Family Questionnaire About Festivals

Dear .....

Your answers to the following questions will be kept confidential and will help us adopt an inclusive and sensitive approach when incorporating the celebration of festivals into our Persona Doll stories and related activities. We will not be telling the children that any religious practices are the 'right' ones or that everyone has to have a religion but will say things like, 'Some people believe that ... but other people don't' or 'In Sally's family they believe ...'

If you would like to discuss this questionnaire with us, please feel free to do so.

- On a scale of 1-10, how important are festivals to your family?

- Which festivals, if any, do you celebrate?

- If you do, how do you celebrate them?

- How do you feel about your festivals being celebrated in our setting?

- How would you like us to support/reflect your festivals?

Gathering this kind of information raises our awareness so we are less likely to assume that everyone from a particular cultural group celebrates certain festivals or that they all celebrate them in the same way.

Celebrating festivals can be sociable and non-threatening occasions. Once parents participate they are more likely to want to take part in celebrating festivals from a wide range of cultures. Celebrating festivals together allows them to share their knowledge and come together socially. It could be the first time that Black parents and White, non-disabled parents and those with disabilities meet each other in a social setting.

These goals are adapted from those proposed by Julie Bisson (1997:36-37):

- **To promote connections among children, families and practitioners**
  Festival celebrations can build and strengthen connections between home and school, and among children and/or practitioners who share the same festivals. They can also promote a sense of community among children as they learn about one another's festivals and participate in activities together.

- **To learn about important events in the lives of all the children and families**
  Introducing festivals that are important to children and their families communicates respect and a commitment to be inclusive. These festival activities enable children and adults to learn about these important events.

- **To support and validate the experiences of children, their families and practitioners**
  Festival activities support children's experiences at home and in their communities and thus strengthen positive feelings about and connections to their family and cultural group. Children get the message that what they do at home is valid – especially valuable for children and families whose festivals are generally not reflected in the media, in shop decorations, in children's books.

- **To reinforce connection to cultural roots**
  Rituals can reaffirm or deepen connections to cultural roots, helping to teach or remind children of who they and their families are – giving them a sense of security. They feel comfort in knowing that they will see some familiar sights, taste some

familiar foods, and be together with people who are important to them.

- **To celebrate both similarities and differences in the children's lives**
  Festival activities can show children in direct, meaningful ways that people often celebrate different festivals honouring events and beliefs unique to their ethnic group. Activities can also point out to children the similar themes that run through many festivals, such as renewal, light and darkness, liberation and harvest.

- **To stretch children's awareness and empathy**
  Learning about a range of festivals is one way to help children move away from ethnocentrism to awareness of other people's lifestyles. Using the Dolls to describe the different ways in which festivals are celebrated can encourage children to share how they celebrate in their own homes and to realise that this isn't the one right or only way.

Our settings may have children whose families are Jehovah's Witnesses and don't celebrate any festivals, Muslim families who do not want their children exposed to any activities related to Easter, and Jewish families who don't want theirs to participate in Christmas activities. This presents us with a challenge. Our commitment to fairness, respect and inclusion means finding viable solutions that meets the needs of every family.

- We could talk to the families, tell them about the Persona Doll stories we intend telling and the creative activities we are planning to do with the children.

- Find out from parents what would and wouldn't be acceptable.

- Keep an open mind and try to see the situation from their perspective. Work out strategies together – it isn't fair to expect the families who don't want their children to participate to come up with all the answers.

- Use a Doll to tell a story about why its family doesn't celebrate a specific festival and another one to explain why its family doesn't celebrate any. Children who celebrate are given simple practical information about the beliefs and practices of those who don't. Having a Doll with a similar identity can relieve some of the isolation that children who don't celebrate might feel. It also relieves the pressure of having to explain why they are not celebrating.

- Use a Jewish Doll to show how it felt when only Christmas was celebrated at its school and some children teased it for not doing so.

- Provide a range of alternative open-ended activities accessible to all the children so that no child feels excluded or bad for not engaging in the holiday activities.

- We may have to limit activities to discussions, reading books and inviting parents to come in and talk about the way they celebrate festivals – they may be persuaded to tell a Persona Doll story!

Welcoming parents into our settings, listening to their views and building relationships based on respect and trust can increase their confidence in leaving their children in our care. The more we consult parents and keep them in touch with the Dolls and their stories, the more successfully we can positively influence their children's attitudes and behaviour.

7

Working with Persona Dolls

The links between the approach advocated by Vygotsky and Bruner and Persona Doll methodology are discussed in this chapter. Also addressed are issues around unequal power relations and implementing anti-discriminatory practice. Supportive documents and legislation that reflect a commitment to equity and justice are cited and a checklist at the end of the chapter gives practitioners an opportunity to evaluate their practice.

P
ractitioners, particularly those implementing anti-discriminatory practice, regard young children not simply as passive recipients of information but as active learners able and willing to strive for fairness and justice. When practitioners actively encourage children to participate in their own learning during Persona Doll storytelling sessions, they are using the approach advocated by both Vygotsky and Bruner. Vygotsky argues that children's learning and development is maximized when children are actively engaged with their environment. He claims that they have the capacity to construct knowledge about their world, that knowledge grows from dialogue and communication with adults and other children that *'the child is a social being whose competencies are interwoven with the competencies of others'* (Bruner and Haste 1987:11).

Vygotsky uses the term 'zone of proximal development (ZPD)' to describe the gap between what children understand or are able to do alone, and the 'zone of actual development (ZAD)' to describe what they achieve with the help of someone more knowledgeable than themselves – adults or other children. There is a transfer of ability from a more competent person to the child. *'What the child can do in co-operation today he can do alone tomorrow'* (Vygotsky 1962/ 1988:41). The adult's role in fostering learning and development is an active one and involves helping children explore beyond their current levels of knowledge and ability and providing support when they tackle new problems. When acting as facilitators during Persona Doll storytelling sessions practitioners encourage children to express their feelings and ideas and extend their knowledge base. During these interactive collaborative sessions children develop their ability to think critically and problem solve.

Like Vygotsky, Bruner believes that cognitive performance is heightened by giving children opportunities to develop original, creative ways of thinking in imaginative situations. Building on Vygotsky's ideas, Bruner (1975) introduced the concept of 'scaffolding' to describe the guidance and support that help a child take the next step for her/himself. It is a process that includes asking open-ended questions, modelling, encouraging children to try dif-ferent approaches and to experiment. When working with Persona Dolls we do this by adjusting our help in response to children's current performance – aiming to reduce our support until they can act alone. So that we can help them move to increased competence we observe them carefully to find out what they can do without our assistance. We ask ourselves what we have seen them do before, how much help they need to reach their goals and what interactions with us will keep them focused.

When children achieve cognitive competence in a particular skill, understanding or disposition they are, in Vygotsky's famous phrase, 'standing a head taller'. Once cognitive competences have been developed in a social context these are internalised, and our guidance and support are no longer needed. However, there will be new com-petences for children to practise and for us to scaffold. In our roles as facilitators during Persona Doll storytelling sessions, for example, we provide the 'scaffolding' in a context that is familiar and meaningful but also challenging. By questioning, prompting, prais-ing, confirming and modelling we extend children's level of under-standing – we build on what they already know and they gain greater competence through describing, explaining and justifying their thinking. The structure of the storytelling sessions enables practitioners to strike a balance between child-initiated and adult-directed interventions and, even if differing and incorrect views are being expressed, communication within the group can produce positive learning. The talk is not just between the children and us but also between the children. Numerous opportunities are provided for interactive problem-solving between adults and children and between children and children.

Language matters

Language plays a fundamental role in the development of learning and understanding. It is through language and social interaction that adults transmit knowledge and societal values to children. Vygotsky (1978) and Bruner (1983) place language, communication and instruction at the heart of intellectual and personal development. Vygotsky advises adults to stimulate children to use language that describes, explains and justifies their thinking because higher cognitive processes develop through communication and dialogue with others. If we accept this close relationship between thought and language we will value scaffolding as being particularly effective for extending children's cognitive and linguistic competence. Participating actively in Persona Doll storytelling sessions and engaging children in a wide variety of creative activities provide the conditions in which children can develop intellectually.

However, McCollom and Blair (1994:98-99) warn that scaffolding is likely to be a more complex and difficult process with some children with disabilities.

> For children who may initiate interactions less frequently, such as those with Down's Syndrome or visual impairment, the adult's role may require more aggressive recruitment. Thus, for the child with a disability, the appropriate balance of support and challenge may look quite different from that which is appropriate to a child who frequently initiates and independently pursues encounters with object or events in his environment.

It is largely through language that adults and children formulate and express their thoughts and make sense of their world but, as Brown (1998) reminds us, the way people speak influences our assessment and response to them.

> ... how people speak 'classifies' them i.e. it reveals their class and ethnic background and where they come from as surely as the clothes they wear or the neighbourhood they live in. Judgements that are based on the way colleagues, children and parents speak influence, often unconsciously, how we relate to and communicate with them. From a linguistic point of view all community languages are equal... It is factually incorrect to describe some languages, for example, Spanish or Swedish as 'better' or 'more developed' than Chinese or Creole. Nevertheless, European languages like French, German and Italian are accorded a higher status than Arabic, Hindi or Swahili. Nevertheless languages spoken by White people continue to be considered superior to languages spoken by Black people, for example, European languages like French, German and Italian are accorded a higher status than Arabic, Hindi or Swahili. (Brown 1998:69-70)

When we tell Persona Doll stories we can acknowledge and promote the cultural and linguistic heritage of every child, foster respect for languages other than their own and encourage the expression of creative, cognitive and linguistic skills in their home language and/or in English. We need to ensure that any names of the Dolls and members of their family which are unfamiliar to the children are correctly pronounced and that the appropriate forms of address are used.

Edwards (1995:6) reminds us that whether bilingualism is viewed as a problem depends on who the children are:

> Bilingualism has not proved to be a problem for children from English speaking homes attending Welsh schools or French immersion programmes in Canada. The critical difference between French-English and Welsh-English bilinguals, on the one hand, and Bengali-English or Panjabi-English bilinguals, on the other is that, in one case, the children learning an additional language belong to a high status group and, in the other, they come from a low status group.

Black children who are learning English as an additional language may experience the response that Cecile Wright (1991:19) noted in her study of children's day to day experience in four schools:

> In the nursery units children came together as a group every day for 'story time' and language work. Through effective discussion and questioning, the teacher encouraged the children to extend their spoken English through, for example, talking about stories and songs. The Asian children were generally excluded from these discussions because it was assumed that they could not understand or speak English. On the occasions when they were encouraged to participate teachers often communicated with them using basic telegraphic language. When this strategy failed to get any response they would quickly lose patience with the children and would then ignore them.

We need to think carefully about how we include children who are learning English as an additional language when we tell Persona Doll stories. The following account is part of a study by Rose Drury (1997) on the home and school experiences of Nazma and her sister.

> Nazma is nearly four years old. Her mother tongue is Phari (a Panjabi dialect spoken by people originating from the Khotli area of Azad Kashmir, which borders north-east Pakistan). She has been at nursery in Britain for seven weeks. At first, none of the monolingual nursery staff talk to Nazma (except for classroom management purposes) and there is no verbal interaction with other children in the nursery (apart from her sister). The only member of staff she is able to understand and with whom she can communicate is the bilingual classroom assistant, Mrs Raja. ... Nazma has a rich family life with daily contacts with five older siblings, parents and grandparents. ... Religious and cultural values are conveyed through family conversation, the stories she hears and her contacts with parents and grandparents. ... She is fully occupied with learning in the home context, and she is encouraged to participate as a member of the family in many ways. But these are not necessarily ways that will prepare her for the expectations in a British nursery setting. For example, she is not encouraged to draw and paint, she does not have bedtime stories read to her, she does not play with construction toys, and she is not used to being asked what she thinks about a topic. Yet such activities and responses will be central to the culture of her nursery. (Rose Drury 1997)

This case study gives food for thought. What strategies could we adopt to ensure that children like Nazma feel comfortable during a Persona Doll storytelling session? How could we prevent the rest of the group from adopting a superior attitude not only towards her but also to her language i.e. looking down on her for not being able to speak English like they can?

As language plays an important role in maintaining cultural identity, oppressive governments frequently forbid the use of languages other than the dominant one. For example, we may be surprised to find that Kurdish children in our group are able to speak Turkish but not their own language. The storytelling sessions provide opportunities to respect and value languages other than English. A Persona Doll from a bilingual 'family' could be used to provide support for children learning English as an additional language and to counter any negative attitudes children may have learnt to languages other than English. Stories also need to be told about Dolls who are fluent in their own language plus English, to highlight the skill of children who are able to speak two or more languages.

Unequal power relationships

Many Persona Doll stories involve unequal power relationships – for instance, boys refuse to let girls play with them; White children tease Black children and call them names. Through the stories children can learn how to be equal partners rather than determining the rules and controlling what happens. When we as practitioners encourage children to consider unfair situations and challenge them, we need to know and appreciate how power relations operate on an individual and institutional level. Josie Levine (1996:111) observed that working class children have a poor deal, *'because the educational base has always been a diverse, class-ridden system promoting the type of education most accessible to the dominant power group and in which, broadly speaking, achievement has depended on pupils originating in the middle classes'*.

Discussions about being in unequal power relationships can help us gain insight into our own and other people's feelings and increase our understanding of how privilege and power – or the lack of them

– affects our lives and the lives of other people. By questioning how power is distributed in society, who profits and who loses out, we can develop strategies to ensure that children are empowered and that those in groups with greater power learn to share their power with others.

Empowering children includes promoting positive attitudes, co-operative friendships and curiosity about the world around them. It involves encouraging them to make up their own minds about what is fair and unfair, to listen to each other, think critically and to take action against inequality and injustice. The ways in which we empower children will depend on the inequalities they encounter. For example, the experiences of Black children, boys, girls and children with disabilities are all different from one another and will need to be empowered in different ways. But as Derman-Sparks (1989:x) suggests, for children to be empowered they each need to acquire particular knowledge, skills and attitudes:

> Empowerment for children of colour requires that they develop strong self-identity and a proud and knowledgeable group identity to withstand the attacks of racism. In contrast, White children's task is to develop a positive identity without White ethnocentrism and superiority. Girls need to learn that they can be competent in all areas and can make choices about their lives. Boys need to learn competence without learning to feel and act superior to girls. The developmental tasks of children with disabilities include learning to use alternative abilities and to gain skills for countering societal practices that sabotage their opportunities for growth. Able-bodied children's tasks include learning ease with differently able people and how to resist stereotyping.

Persona Doll storytelling sessions enable children to become critical co-explorers with practitioners – in the process both are empowered.

Deconstruction – taking apart – is a form of critical thinking through which power relations can be examined. By questioning concepts and meanings that are usually taken for granted, the groups that benefit are revealed and can thus motivate people to do something to change the situation. It is a strategy easily incorporated into our

Persona Doll storytelling sessions and creative activities, to deepen children's understanding of what is fair and unfair. They will have the time and opportunities to express their own ideas and consider alternatives offered by us or the other children. Through the stories, we can encourage them to deconstruct, take apart concepts and the meanings they give to words by asking them questions such as:

- What does being rich mean?

- What does being poor mean?

- Who is rich?

- If you are rich, how are you different?

- What other words could we use to describe poor?

If we listen carefully to the children's answers, we can use them to extend their thinking and help them begin to deconstruct their notions of poor and rich.

MacNaughton and Williams (1996) suggest that children's gender attitudes can be taken apart by:

- uncovering what being a girl or boy means to them

- offering children alternative meanings

- examining with children who benefits from assumptions they have about being boys or being girls

- talking with children about the extent to which they understand that boys or girls have more power and the extent to which they think this is fair or unfair.

We can use the same strategies in our Persona Doll storytelling sessions to help the children deconstruct their understanding of disability. The prevailing negative attitudes towards disability reinforce not only feelings of exclusion and hurt the children with disabilities might well have but also the prejudices and misinformation the non-disabled children might have learnt. All children run the risk of constructing a concept of someone with disabilities as someone different, less valued and less valuable. Through the Dolls and their stories we can explore with children the generally accepted view of beauty, for example. Children are likely to equate being beautiful with looking like princesses in traditional stories. Their faces are beautiful and their bodies are absolutely perfect – this construction of beauty allows for no visible impairment. Stories such as Peter Pan portray people with disabilities as being bad and frightening. Omitting any images of people with disabilities or portraying them negatively can seriously affect disabled children's self-image as well as their perceptions of their own bodies. Non-disabled children and those with disabilities learn what being beautiful means and that the alternative is being ugly. Deconstructing their view of beauty and ugliness includes asking questions like:

- How do you know that someone is beautiful?

- Can people with no legs be beautiful?

- Is it fair to say some people are beautiful and some are ugly?

- How do you think calling people ugly makes them feel?

- Can we be friends with people we call ugly?

During storytelling sessions we can help children to deconstruct concepts of body size, shape and weight and encourage them to respect physical diversity and be proud of their own bodies. In a similar way we can take apart their understanding of racial and cultural stereotypes by uncovering, for instance, what they mean when they use terms like Black and White and to think about what it means to be Black or White.

Equality in practice

Anti-discriminatory practice requires us to be sensitive, sympathetic, flexible and well-informed. We respect and value children as unique individuals, expect each to blossom and to respond co-operatively to adults and other children. Where discriminatory practice is challenged and an antiracist, multicultural, multilingual approach prevails, everyone benefits. Jane Lane (1999:6) urges us to adopt this approach:

> People who work with children do the best for all the children in their care. Most people would like the world to be a place where issues of

equality were irrelevant, a world where everyone already has an equal place in society. ... Our concern here is with young children. They are the most vulnerable members of our society, and everyone working with them needs to strive for them all to be given an equal chance to succeed and fulfil their dreams.

We have a responsibility to help children challenge unfairness and inequality in their lives and the lives of those about them. Discriminatory interactions between children and between practitioners and children should not be permitted and should never be ignored. The perpetrator(s) need to be helped to realise the hurtful consequences of their words and/or actions. The victim(s) need support, comfort and reassurance that the biased interaction was not their fault, that it was not due to any inadequacy on their part.

Refugee children may have endured stressful experiences in their home country and in the UK. Time spent in high quality early years settings can be invaluable, especially for those who have fled a war zone, repression or organised violence. Evidence suggests that most young refugees will benefit from the security of a setting where they can make friends, learn skills, grow in confidence and develop their own identity. They may be withdrawn at first and appear overwhelmed by the noise and the unfamiliar sights and smells. Some will just observe; others may be disruptive and aggressive. Various approaches and strategies may be required to give these children the emotional support they need, help them deal with their feelings and gain their trust and confidence.

To empower children with disabilities to participate to their maximum potential, non-disabled adults and children must actively display non-discriminatory attitudes and their understanding of disability.

Questions like the following can establish whether anti-discriminatory principles are incorporated in all the policies and practices in our settings and whether they are being implemented:

- Are the admission procedures fair?

- Do the children in the setting represent the communities in the area?

- Are all children treated as individuals and with equal concern?

- Do the recruitment, selection and appointment procedures of practitioners meet equality criteria?

- Do all practitioners receive equal treatment and promotion opportunities?

A pertinent question is posed by Mosley (1993): '*Until we promote better relationships, behaviour and self-esteem for the staff, how can we promote it in children?*' Her checklist draws attention to a number of areas that may be creating tensions, distress and frustration.

Assessing the self-esteem and behaviour of practitioners adapted from Jenny Mosley's checklist

Is there a lot of back-biting among practitioners?	
Is there a general lack of support and helpfulness between practitioners?	
Is name-calling, teasing or other forms of verbal abuse experienced by practitioners, ignored?	
Are some practitioners treated less fairly than others?	
Are put downs about one another commonly used as a means of criticism?	
Do practitioners rarely experience praise from each other and from senior staff?	
Do practitioners lack opportunities to put forward their views and express their feelings?	
Do practitioners feel unable to consult other practitioners about personal or work-related problems?	
Are senior members of staff considered unapproachable for help or advice?	
Do practitioners frequently grumble about their workload or responsibilities?	

Thinking about the points she raises could possibly guide us in making changes in relation to our own working environment. But to be effective, management and all members of staff, professional and non-professional, would need to be involved.

Implementing equality in practice involves creating a supportive working environment in which practitioners are given equal opportunities to access in-service training, apply for promotion and have a voice in decision making. In an environment of this kind, genuine efforts are made to meet their needs, their contribution is appreciated and acknowledged and they feel valued members of the team. A spirit of trust, co-operation and mutual respect is fostered so that there is a minimum of back-biting and put-downs.

Caring and kind managers/governors or parents who would not consciously hurt children might in some cases be consciously or unconsciously blocking efforts to implement anti-discriminatory practice. However, embedding equality principles is fast becoming obligatory and no longer a question of individual choice. Documents and legislation like the United Nations Convention on the Rights of the Child (1989), the Children Act (1989), the Report of the Stephen Lawrence Inquiry (1999), and more recently, the Qualifications and Curriculum Authority's (QCA's) Curriculum Guidance for the Foundation Stage (2000), the Human Rights Act (2000), and the Parekh Report of the Commission on the Future of Multi-Ethnic Britain (2000), all require that policy and practice reflect a commitment to equity and justice. These documents offer support to practitioners who work from an anti-discriminatory perspective and oblige others to adopt such an approach. For example: The principles embodied in the UN Convention on the Rights of the Child mirror those that underpin an anti-discriminatory approach. The preamble to this powerful document states that children should be:

> ... brought up in the spirit of the ideas proclaimed in the charter of the United Nations, and in particular in the spirit of peace, dignity, tolerance, freedom, equality and solidarity.

The clauses of most relevance to us are the following:

Articles 1, 2   This Convention applies to everybody up to the age of 18 – to all children and young people whatever their colour, sex, language, national, ethnic or social origin, religion, political opinions, abilities and disabilities.

Article 2   Children and young people who are subject to discrimination or are bullied because of their or their family's position, activity, opinions or religion have the right to protection.

Article 4   Those State Parties that have ratified this Convention shall see to it that the laws and rules of the country correspond to the Convention.
They shall undertake all appropriate measures for the practical implementation of the rights of the child.

Article 22   Children and young people who have been forced to leave their country, alone or together with their family, shall get protection and assistance in the new country. All their rights shall be respected.

Article 23   Children and young people with mental or physical disabilities have the right to live in a way which gives them self-confidence and the possibility to an active life in society.

Article 29   The education of the child shall be directed to:

a.   give the pupil the possibility to develop in his or her own way and according to his or her ability

b.   teach a respect for human rights and freedoms and the principles of the UN, develop respect for the pupil's cultural identity, language and values and for cultures different from his or her own

d   prepare the pupil for a responsible life as an adult in a free society in a spirit of understanding, peace, tolerance, equality of the sexes and friendship among all peoples, teach the pupil respect for the natural environment.

Article 30   Children and young people belonging to a minority or
being indigenous shall have the right to enjoy their own
cultural life. They also have the right to their own
religion and to use their own language.

The passing of the Children Act (1989) was an important milestone.
The Guidance stressed that people working with children needed to
be aware of the very young age at which they learn about, and put
different values on, skin colour, cultures and languages. It also urged
that all provision and practice should enable children to develop
positive attitudes to themselves and other people. The passing of the
Act helped to legitimate the work of organisations like the Early
Years Trainers Anti-Racist Network.

The Report of the Stephen Lawrence Inquiry also draws attention to
the fact that young children learn racist attitudes and behaviour from
an early age.

In his evidence during Part 2 of our enquiry, Chief Constable Burden
(South Wales Police) rightly impressed upon us that racism exists
within all organisations and institutions, and that it infiltrates the community and starts amongst the very young. Recent research in Cardiff
showed that 50% of the racist incidents considered by the Race
Equality Council involved young people under 16 years old, and 25%
of these incidents involved children between the ages of six and ten
years. The problem is thus deeply ingrained. Radical thinking and sustained action are needed in order to tackle it head on, not just in the
Police Services of our country, but in all organisations and in particular
in the fields of education and family life.

...in order to seek to eradicate racism in the longer term, within
society as a whole, the Government should consider how best to empower local education authorities to create, monitor and enforce anti-
racist policies through codes of practice and by amendment of the
National Curriculum, to provide education which deals with racism
awareness and valuing cultural diversity in the multicultural and multi-
ethnic society in which we live. (Macpherson et. al., 1999:33)

When embedded in an anti-discriminatory curriculum, Persona
Dolls and their stories contribute to breaking the cycle by which

White children learn to be racist and Black children suffer – a cycle that has tragic consequences, as the killing of Stephen Lawrence illustrates.

It is good to see that Government policy is acknowledging that anti-discriminatory practice equals good practice – that we can't have the one without the other. In the Curriculum Guidance for the Foundation Stage (2000), some of the suggested principles identified as necessary to achieve high quality care and education in the early years are basic anti-discriminatory principles.

- No child should be excluded or disadvantaged because of his or her 'race', culture or religion, home language, family background, special educational needs, disability, gender or ability.

- Practitioners need to ensure that all children feel included, secure, and valued. They must build positive relationships with parents in order to work effectively with them and their children

- Children, parents and practitioners must work together in an atmosphere of mutual respect.

In the Foreword, Minister Margaret Hodge writes:

> The foundation stage is about developing key learning skills such as listening, speaking, concentration, persistence and learning to work together and co-operate with other children. It is also about developing early communication, literacy and numeracy skills that will prepare children for key stage 1 of the national curriculum.

As part of an anti-discriminatory curriculum, Persona Doll interactive storytelling sessions provide optimum conditions for children to develop these skills.

- Their vocabularies are extended – they are given the words they need to be able to take part in discussions and to think critically.

- They talk about their own experiences, express their ideas, ask questions and listen attentively and respectfully to each other.

- Empathy is fostered by giving them opportunities to talk about the Dolls' feelings and their own. The children care about the Dolls – they are their friends.

- While problem-solving, children are encouraged to think flexibly and critically, visualise a range of realistic solutions, accurately describe a problem and suggest solutions.

- The concepts and language needed to achieve the mathematical development goal and knowledge and understanding of the world are incorporated into the stories.

- The introduction of imaginative, explorative and expressive creative activities ensures that the skills needed to achieve the physical and the creative development goals are achieved.

We may not all support the idea of setting early learning goals but the QCA and the Department for Education and Employment (DfEE) are to be congratulated for stressing these principles. It is admirable that the importance of helping children to recognise their own feelings, empathise with the feelings of others, understand that words and actions can be hurtful, and learn to question and think critically has been highlighted. It would be good if future Guidance also acknowledges that racism damages both Black children and White and that sexism damages both boys and girls. Perhaps it will also actively address the underlying issues and suggest short and long term preventive strategies. *The Parekh Report of the Commission on the Future of Multi-Ethnic Britain* (2000:6) states:

> Whatever its subtle disguises and forms, racism is deeply divisive, intolerant of differences, a source of much human suffering ... It can have no place in a decent society. ... We believe that it is both possible and vitally necessary to create a society in which all its citizens and communities feel valued, enjoy equal opportunities to develop their respective talents, lead fulfilling lives, accept their fair share of collective responsibility, and help create a collective life in which the spirit of civic friendship, shared identity and common sense of belonging go hand in hand with love of diversity.

Using Persona Dolls in an anti-bias curriculum – a checklist

- Do most of the visual images, e.g. pictures and posters, jigsaw puzzles, and board games, feature Black and White, Gypsy/ Traveller, working class and disabled children and their families in a positive way?

- Do the children see images that counter charity posters that often portray adults and children from the 'developing world', or those with disabilities, as people to be pitied?

- Do children often listen to and/or make music derived from a wide range of cultures, thus enabling them to develop their listening skills as well as extending their general knowledge, vocabulary and experience?

- Do the children often have the opportunity of hearing and seeing languages apart from the dominant language? Are a range of languages, especially those spoken by parents and children in the setting, included in the stories and creative activities?

- Do the children have the opportunity to eat foods from many cultures as part of their normal diet and do they make foods from a range of cultures?

- Do the adults actively intervene if children are laughed at, injured or excluded because of the colour of their skin, their physical features, lifestyles, clothes, the languages they speak or their impairments?

- Do the activities and resources reflect and enable the children to learn about all the children and their families in the group and also about the communities living in the area?

- Do the Persona Doll stories we tell, as well as the illustrations and texts in children's books, portray non-stereotypical characters and situations offering children the opportunity to identify with positive and powerful characters in leading roles who are Black and White, Gypsies/Travellers and disabled? Do they show people from these groups living happy and successful lives?

- Do the Dolls we use accurately portray skin tones and physical features?

- Do the Persona Doll stories we tell reflect the lives and lifestyles of all the children in the group?

- Are the Dolls portrayed as victims or as self-respecting and confident 'children' seeking advice and friendship?

- Do the personas we create reinforce stereotypes? Are Black adults and children portrayed as poor and in single-parent families? Are girls depicted as vulnerable and in need of protection while boys are brave and strong?

- Do the personas we create and the stories we tell challenge children's feelings of superiority?

- Do the personas we create and the stories we tell reflect adults and children from a range of ethnic and cultural backgrounds and abilities?

- Do the personas we create and the stories we tell encourage children to have faith in themselves and accept themselves and others as unique individuals?

- Do the personas we create and the stories we tell enable all the children to identify with characters that are self-confident and creative, caring and gentle?

- Do the personas we create and the stories we tell portray men and women, boys and girls expressing a wide range of feelings?

- Do the personas we create and the stories we tell encourage children to take responsibility for their own learning and make up their own minds about issues of fairness and unfairness?

- Do the personas we create and the stories we tell reflect people from class, cultural and ethnic backgrounds that are different from our own without encouraging or reinforcing stereotypical thinking?

- Do the stories and the creative activities develop verbal and non-verbal skills for a range of purposes?

- Do the creative activities enable children to discover and develop different ways to express their ideas and feelings?

- Does the atmosphere contribute to peaceful and enjoyable learning?

It is not generally appreciated or acknowledged by the media or the general public that caring for and expanding the horizons of young children carries enormous responsibilities and requires dedication, knowledge, understanding, and a wide range of skills and experience. The power, influence and responsibility of teachers is encapsulated in the following short passage. It applies to all practitioners working with young children or students.

The Teacher

I have come to the frightening conclusion: I am the decisive element in the classroom. It is my personal approach that creates the climate. It is my daily mood that makes the weather. As a teacher I possess tremendous power to make a child's life miserable or joyous. I can be a tool of torture or an instrument of inspiration. I can humiliate or humour, hurt or heal. In all situations it is my response that decides whether a crisis will be escalated or de-escalated; a child humanised or de-humanised.

Quoted at a conference by Chris Henshaw Barnet's Principal Equalities Adviser 27/10/00.

8

Training with Persona Dolls

This chapter begins with a number of tasks that lecturers and in-service trainers might like to use to highlight anti-discriminatory principles and issues. It goes on to describe a few of the training programmes that have been built around the Dolls.

I have argued throughout this book that Persona Dolls are a powerful tool for countering discrimination and promoting equity and social justice among young children. And that to be fully effective, the Dolls and their stories should be integrated into an anti-discriminatory curriculum and used by people who are skilled, respectful and empathetic. To achieve this goal trainers need constantly to evaluate their own attitudes and practices and be willing and able to make changes, while practitioners and students require training to understand the principles on which an anti-discriminatory approach is based. Accordingly, this chapter begins with a number of anti-discriminatory exercises to link with issues raised in the book. Lecturers and in-service trainers should find these exercises useful and be able to adapt them to meet their own particular situations. Further ideas and support are provided in the examples of Persona Doll training programmes.

Raising awareness about racism and other forms of discrimination calls for sensitivity, knowledge, skill and experience. White participants, especially if they have only recently become involved in challenging racism, may not realise, for example, that talking about race often evokes strong emotional responses and influences the reactions of Black participants who already feel vulnerable. White trainers need to offer support and at the same time help the White participants acknowledge and empathise with the pain, frustration and anger felt by Black people confronted yet again with racism.

Trainers no longer antagonise, alienate and make participants feel guilty, defensive and angry as sometimes happened in the 1970s. Now the emphasis is on changing attitudes through understanding where people are positioned and why they think and act the way they do. The concern is with learning how to analyse problems, work out strategies and then take action.

During training sessions trainers have been surprised and delighted at the way adults empathise and respond to the Dolls, especially those who have had the advantage of previous anti-discriminatory training.

Anti-discriminatory training

■ AGREEING TERMS

- **In small groups, participants suggest which terms they like other people to use when referring to their ethnic origin, gender and/or abilities and the terms they dislike. They give their reasons for their preferences and objections.**

- **When the group reaches a consensus one of them lists the terms under two headings: Preferred – Unacceptable. Any terms about which there is still disagreement are recorded under a separate heading. The results are shared in the feedback session.**

Note to the trainer: This task may arouse strong feelings about the acceptability of particular terms. Participants may need to be reminded that they should listen to and respect the views of others even if they don't accept them, and be sensitive to the fact that some terms cause pain. Providing an historical context can help to explain the reason(s) for this.

In the feedback session the preferred and unacceptable terms on which participants agree are listed on a flipchart or board. Terms on which there is no agreement are likely to trigger further discussion.

■ IS IT A FACT?

- Each participant writes down three statements that describe each of the following categories – men, women, Black people and people with disabilities.

- The trainer asks for volunteers to contribute their descriptions and enters them on a flipchart or board under the appropriate headings.

- The group decides which of the descriptions are factual statements and which are stereotypes and they give reasons for their choices. These are listed under the headings: Factual statements and Stereotypes.

- From this discussion the group agrees on the difference between a statement of fact and a stereotype.

Note to the trainer: Some participants may express misgivings about doing the task because they oppose stereotyping groups of people. Others may be upset by some of the statements claiming to describe their group. The feelings which are expressed can be used to encourage empathy with other stereotyped groups and raise awareness about the hurt that stereotypical thinking can cause.

Participants are likely to conclude that facts need to be supported by evidence – stereotypes do not. For example, it is a fact that men and women are biologically different. There is no evidence to support the stereotype that the genders differ intellectually.

Participants might appreciate the opportunity to share how they felt when they were stereotyped and how they reacted.

■ TO ACT OR NOT TO ACT

In small groups, participants talk about a racist incident they witnessed, why they think it was racist and what they did or didn't do in response. Some incidents may be clearly identifiable as racist, while others may be less obviously. When everyone has contributed, the groups to consider the obstacles that stopped them from acting.

Note to the trainer: It is important to point out the obvious difference between being the observer and being the target of racism. It is vital that everyone is sensitive to how this task might make Black members of the group feel and give them support.

The Stephen Lawrence Inquiry Report described a racist incident as, 'any incident which is perceived to be racist by the victim or any other person'.

Incidents might involve:

> Discrimination
> Exclusion
> Harassment
> Physical attack/verbal abuse
> Stereotyping
> Racist jokes
> Patronising attitude(s)
> Being marginalised/ignored

Obstacles to action:

*   People are often taken by surprise, not by the fact that racism exists, but because it suddenly hits them out of the blue and at the time they can't think what to say or do.

*   Anger, distress, fear of confrontation, fear that they won't be liked, fear of being isolated, fear of being ridiculed, fear of physical retaliation – all these fears add up to a powerful package of social dynamics that often prevent people from acting.

*   Being the only person who appears to be affected by the incident.

- Being unwilling to stick one's neck out.

- Been socialised not to 'interfere', to mind one's own business.

Whether to act or not to act is likely to be influenced by the incident itself, by prevailing conditions and by the personality and feelings of the person who witnessed it.

The following story was used by a trainer who had given participants an exercise to decide whether incidents were racist or not. It could be used to trigger further discussion:

The Giant Steps[1]

Once upon a time, in a land far away, there lived an enormous giant. He was at least ten feet tall, with a mop of red hair and a beard. In his hand he carried a big axe. Every year, on the same day, at the same time, the giant would walk down from the mountains which were his home to stand outside the walls of the town, terrorising the people inside.

'Send me your bravest man and I will fight him,' the giant would shout, 'Send me someone to fight or I will knock down your walls and kill everyone.'

And every year the gate would slowly open and fearfully some valiant soul would walk out to meet the giant and certain death.

And every year the poor wretch would stand mesmerised by the size of the giant and the impossible task. Not one person had even managed to draw his sword before the giant crushed him with one blow of his fist and then finished him with his axe.

One day a young traveller arrived in the town.

'Why does everyone look so frightened and miserable?' he asked.

One of the townsfolk told him the story of the yearly visit of the giant and the yearly slaying of the person who went out to fight.

---

1. *From Tales for Trainers: using stories and metaphors to facilitate learning* by Margaret Parkin, Kogan Page, 1998.

'It's as though they are hypnotised. The giant crushes them where they stand. They don't even draw their sword.'

Just then the traveller heard the giant,

'Send me your bravest man and I will fight him.'

'I am here,' said the traveller throwing open the gate and striding towards him. For a moment they stood and faced each other. Although the giant was still a long way away from the traveller, the giant's sheer size and shocking appearance struck him as very curious.

As he walked towards the giant, concentrating on his eyes and his shock of hair and huge beard he realised that instead of getting bigger the giant began to shrink before his eyes until he was no more than a foot tall. With one quick thrust he plunged his sword into the giant's heart.

As he lay dying the traveller bent down and whispered, 'Who are you?' With his dying breath he replied,

'My name is Fear.'

Participants at the training session were asked what the story meant to them. These are some of the responses:

- The giant represents our fear of facing racism.

- The giant is racism.

- When you face your fears they are not so gigantic after all and you can overcome them.

- When you take action the fear disappears.

■ COLOUR MATTERS

Ahmed is the only Black boy in an infant class. The teacher gives each of the children pale pink card. She tells them that it is soon going to be Mother's Day and they are going to make cards for their mothers. They must first draw a picture of their mother on the front of the card and then write a message on the back.

In small groups, participants to consider the following scenario:

Ahmed: My mum isn't pink. She's brown. Can I have a brown card?

Vivien: I don't like brown – it's yucky!

Joshua: Mucky brown, yucky brown

Pakki, Pakki, Pakki brown

The children take up the chant. Ahmed puts his hands over his ears.

Teacher: That's enough! Get on with your drawing.

All do except Ahmed, who continues to protest.

Teacher: Ahmed, stop fussing and do what you're told. Just pretend that your mum is pink for today.

Reluctantly, Ahmed picks up his pencil and begins to draw.

- Suggest what effect the incident could have on Ahmed and on the other children

- Decide whether this was a racist incident.

- How could it have been handled differently?

Note to the trainer: It is important to be sensitively aware of the feelings that this exercise might arouse for Black participants as a result of their own or their children's experiences. If possible speak with them in advance about the reasons for the session and what you hope will come out of it. Convey this sensitivity to the White participants.

Possible responses:

Ahmed probably felt angry, frustrated, confused, isolated, put down. The other children were likely to feel that their skin colour was 'better' than Ahmed's, especially because the teacher provided only pink card.

It is a racist incident because the teacher reinforced the belief that pinkish skin is superior – and, furthermore, that it is the norm. Telling Ahmed to pretend that his mum was pink suggests that skin colour doesn't matter, which is clearly not the case in racist Britain. The children were being given a negative message about diversity and difference. By not dealing with their chanting the teacher indicated that such behaviour was acceptable.

An alternative response

The teacher listens to Ahmed, and acknowledges that his reaction is justified. She apologises and provides him with the appropriate colour card. She explains to all the children why Vivien's remark and Joshua's chant are hurtful and unacceptable. The incident might not have happened had she provided a variety of cards from which the children could choose the one they thought best matched the colour of their mother's skin. This could encourage children to compare and talk about the similarities and differences in skin colour in a positive context.

Trainers might find this poem by an anonymous pupil from King Edward VI school Handsworth Birmingham a useful way to end this exercise.

Coloured!

Dear White Fella	You White Fella
coupla tings you should know	When you born, you pink
When I born, I black	When you grow up, you white
When I grow up, I black	When you go in the sun, you red
When I go in the sun, I black	When you cold, you blue
When I cold, I black	When you scared, you yellow
When I scared, I black	When you sick, you green
When I sick, I black	And when you die, you grey.
And when I die	And you have the cheek
I still black.	to call me coloured!

■ TEACHER ALWAYS KNOWS BEST?

A teacher takes her reception class for the first time to the hall for music and movement. She tells them to take off their clothes but to leave their vests and pants on. They excitedly begin to undress. The teacher, greatly agitated, rushes over to Prema, the only Asian child.

Teacher: I didn't mean you, Prema. You know you mustn't take your clothes off. Your mum and dad will be very cross with me if I let you undress like the other children.

Prema: No they won't.

Teacher: Come on, everybody's waiting for you.

Bewildered and upset, Prema joins the other children.

The next morning a discussion takes place between Prema's parents, the headteacher and Prema's teacher.

Note to the trainer: Role-plays may not be popular but they are extremely useful. They enable people to practice being in a particular situation and in someone else's shoes and they also present the opportunity to try out using actual words that could be used. People are often reluctant at first to take part so if nobody volunteers, take on one of the roles yourself.

- Participants role-play the encounter between the parents, the headteacher and the teacher.

- To explore the various ways in which the situation might be handled, the role-play is enacted a number of times with different people taking part. The rest of the group act as observers.

Feedback

The players comment on why they behaved as they did when in role and how they felt. The observers talk about their reactions to each of the role-plays.

■ LEARNING FROM PARENTS

- Members of the group are to offer constructive suggestions to a childminder who has just been registered. Parents who are practising Rastas will be coming to talk to her about the possibility of her caring for Ashan, their 2 year old son. She is keen to build a partnership with them and believes that parents usually know more than anyone about their own children and have very definite ideas about how they want them to be brought up.

- What will she need to do to convince Ashan's parents that she will provide the care they want?

- What information will they need to give her?

Possible responses:

Childcare

They should all discuss and come to agreement about the preparation and eating of food. Any dietary restrictions should be identified. Parents need to tell her how they discipline Ashan and about his sleep and personal hygiene routines. For example, whether he uses a potty, has a comforter or a special toy that he might like to bring with him.

Identity issues

Parents need to give the preferred name of their son because it is closely linked to his identity. It is important that the childminder uses it and does not shorten or substitute it with an anglicised name. If she finds his name unfamiliar, the childminder needs to practice pronouncing it until she feels confident using it. Language is also closely tied up with identity. If Ashan's home language is not English, she should learn a few words, some rhymes and songs in his first language.

Cultural practices

Before meeting the parents the childminder should find out all she can about Rastafarianism from the library and from members of the local Rasta community, if there is one.

She can show acceptance, appreciation and respect for artefacts from the parent's culture by asking them if they would like to bring in some to help Ashan feel at home. She needs to ensure that she provides books and toys in which he will see himself reflected.

In this case, the childminder knew that the parents were practising Rastafarians. If she hadn't, she should not have assumed that because the family were from a particular cultural group that they would necessarily carry out all or any of its cultural practices.

Honouring the contract

Once agreement has been reached, she must respect the parents' wishes and stick to them so that a collaborative partnership can be built.

■ 'THEY' NEVER PARTICIPATE!

A letter is sent out to parents telling them that their children will be visiting a farm the following Wednesday. They are asked to ensure that their children will be at the school no later than 8.30am with a packed lunch. The coach will be bringing them back at 3.30pm. It is hoped that as many parents as possible will come on the outing.

- In small groups participants consider the reasons why the only parents who did not send their children on the outing or come themselves were the two from Gypsy/Traveller families.

- Could anything have been done that might have induced them to come?

Note to the trainer: Be particularly sensitive to the feelings of participants who have identified themselves as Gypsies/Travellers and appreciate that others might hide their ethnic origin for fear of prejudice and hostility. It is advisable to assume that there could be at least one Gypsy/Traveller in the group.

Possible responses:

Communication

Some Gypsy/Traveller parents do not read or write – their fear of being found out could prevent their telling the school. Friendly face to face communication is more likely to be effective than a letter. The mothers may not have been able to accompany their children because they have little ones at home. The letter did not say that they could come.

Discrimination

Many Gypsy/Traveller parents have a deep-rooted fear and mistrust of allowing outsiders to supervise their children. This stems from the frequent prejudice, discrimination and harassment they face.

The Gypsy/Traveller mothers may have been afraid of hostility from other parents and stayed away because they didn't feel confident about spending such a long time with them.

Reaching out

Visiting parents or inviting them into school can help to build confidence and trust. Parents need to feel welcome and comfortable and able to see that the practitioners and children respect and acknowledge the many positive aspects of Gypsy/Traveller life. Examples of good practice might include setting up a trailer home corner, and developing themes such as 'working animals' or 'homes' as an integral part of the curriculum.

Raising awareness

Practitioners need to recognise that Gypsies/Travellers are discriminated against on grounds of 'race' and their – asssumed – nomadic lifestyle. They may need training and support to be able to express their feelings and develop the skills and confidence required to create meaningful partnerships with Gypsy/Traveller parents.

■ GIVING A POLICY TEETH

A family centre is due to open in two months time and staff hope to attract Black and White children and those with disabilities. They are about to begin formulating their equality policy. Working in small groups:

- **Consider what steps they should take.**

- **Decide what issues they need to consider.**

- **Suggest practical strategies.**

Possible responses:

Anti-discriminatory practice equals good practice

For the policy to be effective, all those involved need to understand that good practice requires an anti-discriminatory approach.

Owning the policy

The aims must be agreed and supported by everyone working in the setting, including senior management and representatives from the communities it serves. It is a complex process which is affected not only by the attitudes and expectations of everyone involved but also by the relationships between them. A collaborative, constructive, equitable, non-threatening and supportive working atmosphere enables everyone to feel comfortable.

Embedding equality of opportunity and treatment

Equality issues need to be considered within all aspects of the Centre, and staff need to know about and understand the relevant legislation and be able to use it.

Recruitment and selection processes as well as promotion procedures need to be firmly based on equality principles.

Accreditation of prior learning and experience must be taken into account, as well as variations in culture and religion.

The admission procedures need to meet equal opportunity criteria. The policy needs to encourage equality in curriculum planning, design and delivery – the content of what is taught, how it is taught and the promotion of positive images of adults and children need to be thoroughly considered.

Cultural issues

The policy has to take account of the religious practices and dietary requirements of the children and encourage the valuing of languages other than English, sign languages and Braille.

To do this effectively, comprehensive records of all the children need to include not only their full names but also the names they are known by, their ethnicity, the languages they can speak and the first language of their parents.

Disability issues

Ensure that practitioners, parents and children with disabilities can access all parts of the building.

Ensure that children with disabilities have equal access to the curriculum.

Code of practice

If children, practitioners or students encounter discrimination, procedures need to be set up for dealing with the situation

Strategies should be developed for implementing an effective on-going system of monitoring and evaluating the policy.

The procedures for reporting to at least one named person in a senior position must be clearly stated.

The actions that will be taken if the terms of the policy are breached must be agreed and included. Practitioners need to understand that if they persist in behaving in ways that contravene the terms of the policy they could face disciplinary action.

■ NO PROBLEM HERE

Participants divide into groups. Each represents a team of advisers in a local education authority committed to inclusion. A nursery school is causing concern because although ethnic minority families with young children live in the area, they don't attend the school. The staff say that as they have none of 'them', they don't need to bother about antiracist or multicultural education. What needs to be done to change their attitudes and practice?

Note to trainer: Participants may not be aware that wherever children live in Britain they are exposed to racist attitudes and practices. As these can have a negative effect on their development, practitioners have a responsibility to counter this influence.

Participants are likely to suggest that:

• The admission procedures of the school need to be reviewed.

• The ethos and daily programme of the school may be discouraging ethnic minority parents from applying.

• The QCA requires that no child should be excluded or disadvantaged because of his or her race, culture or religion, family background, home language, special educational needs, disability, gender or ability.

• Practitioners need to ensure that all children feel included, secure, and valued. They need opportunities to learn about a range of cultures, develop their curiosity, vocabularly and general knowledge.

■ FOOD FOR THOUGHT – two case studies to consider

Mujo and Aida are twins. They escaped from their village with their mother and came to the UK. They seemed to settle reasonably well at nursery, joining in many of the activities though not always sustaining an interest or developing their play. During free play they are always in the home corner and repeatedly play the following scene:

> They sit at the kitchen table in silence having pretended to make a drink. The telephone is placed on the table with great ceremony. Every now and then Mujo picks it up, has an agitated conversation, throws the phone to the floor and Aida comforts him. This play pattern repeats itself several times a day over some weeks. Their possession of the telephone is beginning to lead to conflict with the other children.

> What do you think their play signifies?
> What do you think the children are feeling?
> Should you intervene?
> How would you do this?

> A 5 year old Kurdish boy was very restless. He wandered around looking at everything appearing to be quite happy. He spoke quite a bit but in a language nobody understood. He had never been to an early years group before. Careful assessment of his language revealed it was a mixture of Turkish, Kurdish and English. He spoke Kurdish for the first couple of years and then had to switch to Turkish when the family moved to a town where speaking Kurdish was forbidden. Just as his Turkish was getting established, he came to the UK and was now picking up English. At home his parents mainly spoke Turkish, some Kurdish and English. His parents want him to speak only English at the nursery. Do you agree with them?

Persona Doll Training Programmes

PERSONA DOLLS: EDUCATION WITHOUT PREJUDICE

Persona Dolls have been successfully used for many years in the USA and Australia but are less well known in this country and in the rest of Europe generally. Through their training project, 'Persona Dolls: education without prejudice', the partners from Denmark, the Netherlands and the UK have turned the spotlight onto Persona Dolls and their contribution to countering racism and other forms of discrimination. Seminars and conferences in the partner countries helped to raise awareness but the main thrust of the project is the work being done with students and practitioners. The project is reported in some detail because it offers practical ideas that can be adapted and implemented by lecturers in colleges and in-service trainers.

In the UK the Dolls were introduced to participating students within an anti-discriminatory framework, and in the first year all staff in day care centres and schools in the Netherlands and Denmark had anti-discriminatory training before becoming involved in the project. This knowledge and experience provided the students and practitioners with a sound basis from which to begin working with the Dolls to develop empathy and challenge the learning of prejudice and discriminatory attitudes. It's interesting that in the Netherlands, participants who joined the project in the second year without the benefit of anti-discriminatory training used the Dolls only to arouse empathy.

Training students

The UK partner focused on two groups of second year CACHE NNEB students at Sutton Coldfield College who were completing a 40-hour module of their Diploma, entitled 'Work with children'. This module includes the short and long term planning of appropriate activities, making and utilising resources to enhance the activities and exploring issues relating to racism, sexism and disability.

Second year students were selected because they have greater experience of storytelling than those in their first year. The tutor hoped that making Persona Dolls would provide opportunities for students to link their theoretical knowledge about anti-discriminatory practice with their hands-on work with children.

The project was launched at a workshop where students were told about the aims of the project, how Persona Dolls are used to combat discrimination, the Danish and Dutch contribution to the project and their part in it. They were surprised and many were delighted to hear that they would be making two 30-inch Dolls – one to be submitted towards their Module B portfolio and then donated to the college and the other for them to keep.

The students were invited to think about the kind of Dolls they wanted to make. They discussed the authenticity of facial features, hair textures and styles and the possibility of creating realistic skin tones by dying fabrics with commercial dyes and experimenting with vegetable dyes such as onion skins. Issues around creating personas for the Dolls were also raised. It was impressed on the students that they should interact appropriately with parents when asking for information about their cultural practices or about the aids their children use, for example, hearing or mobility aids.

The workshop concluded with the group sharing the identities they intended creating for their Dolls and the reasons for their choices.

Over the next few months the students were guided and supported by two lecturers – one overseeing the making of the Dolls and the other (the European partner in the project) ensuring that the facial and physical features and their clothing were as accurate as possible and that the personas and stories created by the students reflected the lives of the children they would be working with. Apart from producing appropriate Dolls, the aim was to extend the students' critical thinking about bias – and their confidence, knowledge and skills. It was felt that the students' views and behaviour could be positively influenced by making and using the Dolls to help young children unlearn discriminatory attitudes.

At the end of the academic year the students produced a really amazing collection of Dolls – a tribute to their own ingenuity and to the guidance and support they received from the lecturers. The project boosted their self-esteem, heightened their awareness of the harm stereotyping causes and the importance of accurately portraying skin colour, physical features and disabilities. Parents generously gave advice and practical help.

Making the Dolls took more time than was anticipated so, unfortunately, the students had little opportunity to use their Dolls with the children. But this miscalculation has been more than compensated for. The college has given Dolls to some of the training placements and the present second year students are enjoying working with them. In response to the interest generated by these students, a workshop was held at the college for teachers who are now using the Dolls with the children.

The second year of the project provided an opportunity to revisit the design of the Dolls. The feedback confirmed that being two and a half feet tall seemed to add to the Dolls' charisma and to the importance of their anti-discriminatory messages. The possibility of arranging for the Dolls to spend weekends in children's homes is being discussed and has raised issues around training and also working with parents and older siblings. The fact that racism and other social inequalities blight the attainment, self-esteem and lives of many young children and their families clearly demonstrates the need for students and practitioners to continue working with the Dolls within an anti-discriminatory framework.

Training practitioners

In the Netherlands and Denmark, the project was also launched at two-day workshops. Here too the emphasis was on anti-discriminatory practice and how the Dolls and their stories could be used to encourage children to respect, value and learn about diversity. Before the workshop the practitioners had been encouraged to observe the children in their group and to note:

- diversity within the group – family structure, skin colour, cultural and linguistic backgrounds

- the attitudes and opinions of colleagues, parents and children – what they say about people who are different from themselves. Do the children tease and call each other names?

- the emotions that children express – anxiety, pleasure, sadness, frustration.

Participants shared their findings and in the useful discussions that ensued, key issues were raised. The aims of the project were explained and the Dolls and their stories introduced. Participants from each of the settings then chose the Doll that most appealed to them from the range provided. Participants at the Dutch workshop were enthusiastic and proud about being involved in a European project. They were apprehensive about working with the Dolls but thought the approach was concrete and inspiring. The response in Denmark was less positive. Over the years they had worked with a variety of dolls to confront various issues and they were not keen to re-invent the wheel! They raised a number of questions, for instance, how many problems could one Doll experience? Their suggestion that Persona Dolls should look different from the dolls children play with in the home corner was later incorporated into the training.

Implementing the project took longer than anticipated because the partners underestimated the need for on-going support and training to boost confidence and allay anxieties. However, once the practitioners started using the Dolls with the children their misgivings, fears and initial resistance began to melt away. Ongoing support and regular workshops enabled everyone to share experiences, celebrate their successes and learn from any 'failures'.

During the second year of the project practitioners from other schools and day care centres were invited to join in. Their integration presented few problems and all the settings are building their collections of Dolls and creating appropriate personas and stories. Participating practitioners feel that the Dolls are special and that they have enriched their work with the children. In general, parents have also reacted positively – they approve of the way the practitioners are tackling discrimination with the help of the Dolls.

On-going monitoring and evaluation of the project was carried out by the partners and by practitioners. As the participating settings in the Netherlands are daycare centres and playgroups, the children range in age from 18 months to 4 years, and the stories tend to be around situations in which the children empathised with the Dolls. It was felt that the project suffered because no older children were involved in it. Nevertheless, the children love the Persona Dolls and are so enthusiastic they recount the stories to their parents.

A positive outcome is that the practitioners are developing their ability to observe the children closely in their settings – listening to what they are saying about and to one another. They are encouraged to draw on their observations at the workshops and when they are creating personas and stories around the Dolls. The practitioners feel that video recording sessions provided them with valuable learning experiences.

LEARNING BY DOING

This Persona Doll training programme is designed to provide hands-on experience, raise awareness and offer opportunities for reflection and discussion of issues as they arise. A group of about 20 people ensures maximum participation.

The training begins with brief personal introductions, agreement on the ground rules and stressing the importance of completing the evaluation form.

❏ Task One

- Think about the faces of one or two of the children in your group (or children you know well). Note down their similarities and the ways they differ

- Note down their group identities, for example: ethnic, gender, class, religious, language, physical disability

- Note down individual differences. For example, family structure, physical appearance (short, tall, fat, thin, birthmarks, glasses)

- Do you see any differences that would cause either or both children to be teased or put down by the other children?

- Do either or both show sensitivity or embarrassment about any aspect of who they are or what they like to do? For example, refusing to speak their home/community language.

❏ Task two

Whole group brainstorm the equality issues in their workplace(s) and the community.

This exercise is followed by a short talk on selecting appropriate dolls and creating personas for them. The main points are briefly listed here. For more detailed discussion, refer to chapters two and three.

- Any Doll can be a Persona Doll – consider why large almost child-size cloth Dolls are preferred

- Persona Dolls are the adults' Dolls not the children's – so they don't live in the home corner

- The importance of avoiding stereotyping when selecting Dolls

- The Dolls need to represent children in the setting without exactly replicating any single child.

- Aim to encourage children to identify and empathise with the Dolls

- Talk about some of the issues around creating personas for the Dolls

Participants are encouraged to ask questions.

Using one of the Dolls, the trainer models introducing a Persona Doll to the participants, who are encouraged to respond as if they were the children.

❏ Task three

In small groups, participants discuss and negotiate which Doll they would like to choose from the range provided. They decide whether the chosen Doll is a boy or a girl and create a detailed persona for it

– its family and cultural background, where it lives, where it sleeps, the language(s) it speaks, the things it can do and those it finds difficult, its likes and dislikes e.g. food, music, games and TV. It is given a name. Participants sometimes find it helpful to draw on the information they provided in task one.

Still in small groups, particpants take turns role-playing being the practitioner introducing the Doll to a group of 'children' i.e. the other participants. As it is the first time the 'children' meet the Doll, the goal at this stage is to encourage them to identify and empathise with it – to become friends.

Feedback: The focus is on:

* how participants felt when creating their Doll's persona and when role-playing

* providing opportunities for participants to make general comments and ask questions.

This feedback is very important because many of the joys and difficulties involved in working with the Dolls are likely to be highlighted.

❏ Task four

The whole group brainstorm situations that could occur during Persona Doll story-telling sessions and suggest strategies for dealing with them.

For example:

* the child who never participates and the one who participates 'too much'

* domestic violence

* unexpected responses to bereavement – such as expressions of anger towards the person who has died.

❏ Task five

We need to think carefully about how we respond to children who are learning English as an additional language.

In small groups imagine that Suyuan who is $4^1/_2$ has been in your setting for six weeks. Her mother tongue is Chinese, which neither you nor the other children can speak. They seldom attempt to make contact with her but she responds to your efforts to involve her in ongoing activities. When her parents or grandparents come to fetch her, her face brightens and she chatters animatedly with them.

You are about to tell your group of ten children a Persona Doll story and will be reinforcing the main points of the story through a creative activity.

• What strategies will you adopt to help make Suyuan comfortable and the rest of the group respond to her positively?

Feedback: Enables participants who work with children learning English as an additional language to extend their knowledge base and to share their expertise. This can be a significant learning experience for participants who work with children who speak only English.

❏ Task six

Think of an incident when you were discriminated against as a child. (If you can't recall one, then please draw, if you can, on an adult experience). Then share the incident and how you felt with your neighbour.

Brief feedback to the group.

This exercise is followed by a short talk on the importance of using the Dolls in an anti-discriminatory context. Next, the trainer models a story that raises an anti-discriminatory issue – the participants again responding as children.

❏ Task seven

• In the same groups as before, discuss how you would present your Doll and the questions you would ask about it to refresh the children's memories.

• Work out how you would introduce and develop an anti-discriminatory story – perhaps around an incident you have witnessed in your workplace or experienced as a young child.

Could draw on the equality issues listed at the beginning of the day. Specify age group, and think about what you hope children will gain – include the skills and attitudes children need to acquire in order to achieve the Early Learning Goals.

- You will also need to consider how you would wind up the session.

- In your own group, take turns in the role of the practitioner while the rest are the children – remember it is an interactive session so the 'children' need to respond appropriately. When you are presenting the Doll, imagine you are telling the story to the group of children/students you work with.

- Agree who the practitioner will be when role-playing in the large group.

- If there is time, suggest how you would follow up the story-telling session with creative activities that extend and build on the issues raised in the story and the achievement of the creative development goals. The aim is to reinforce the knowledge, skills and attitudes the children have learned and to deepen their awareness and sensitivity.

Feedback: After each small group has performed its role-play to the whole group, participants talk about their feelings when they were the practitioners and the children and share any issues that arose. They also suggest what skills, knowledge and attitudes children could develop from the storytelling session to help them achieve the Early Learning Goals. The creative activities that were suggested are shared.

The next task is introduced and the situation is role-played in the large group – if nobody volunteers, the trainer could encourage them by volunteering to take one of the roles.

❏ Task eight

Upset and angry parents have come into your setting to complain about a Persona Doll story you've told the children. Agree the issue (for example, the story from the previous task or the scenario from task five could be used) and decide who will role-play the parent(s), member of staff and the Head/Manager to the whole group. The rest of the group to be observers.

The feedback to include general discussion.

❏ Task nine

Please share with your neighbour two of the steps you will take to introduce the Dolls into your workplace.

Training ends with the reading of the children's book, *Something Else* (1994) by Kathryn Cave and the completion of evaluation forms.

As the Persona Doll approach is new and innovative, practitioners tend to welcome training, feeling that they lack the skills and confidence to get it right. Training has been found to motivate and empower them. Participants show high levels of interest and many report positive effects in terms of their personal development and self-awareness – as the following comments from evaluation forms illustrate:

> 'Thought-provoking – made me appreciate that using the Dolls will require a lot of thought and planning but feel that the results would be rewarding.'

> 'I think I am less likely to reinforce stereotypes and feel more confident about choosing culturally appropriate Dolls that mirror the children in my group.'

> 'After much more thought and very careful planning and discussion I would be able to use Persona Dolls very sensitively.'

> 'The practical tasks were hard. I feel I need to work on my confidence but the potential of the Dolls is so great I feel that it will be well worth using the ideas and methods.'

Following training, a group of Community Teachers, Area Planners and members of the Training and Quality Team in Sheffield came together to plan the Foundation Stage/Early Learning Goals training for eligible providers in the city. Persona Dolls were used as part of the Personal, Social and Emotional Development element of this training. The planning team felt that the Dolls were especially useful for developing the PSED 'clusters'. The training is being delivered using Persona Dolls to over 100 eligible providers in the city. Feedback on this training has so far been very positive.

Persona Doll training is designed to provide participants with the knowledge, skills and confidence they need to promote equality and justice when working with the Dolls.

Bringing about change isn't easy. Oppressions are deeply rooted and interlinked but the good news is that through using the Dolls in the context of a culturally and anti-discriminatory curriculum we can contribute to the elimination of social inequality.

9

Creative learners

The focus of this chapter is on how the anti-discriminatory messages that we transmit to children during storytelling sessions can be reinforced through creative and imaginative activities. A number are suggested to assess and expand children's understanding and to enable them to experience a sense of achievement and feel good about themselves.

By suggesting activities designed to reinforce and build on Persona Doll storytelling sessions, I invite accusations of teaching my grandmother to suck eggs! Providing creative and imaginative activities is part and parcel of the daily programme in all settings, so my suggestions will be familiar to practitioners particularly to those who are implementing anti-discriminatory theory and practice. When planning our overall provision and providing activities, we need to be sensitive to the feelings of every child. We need to check that Black children, refugees, Traveller children, those not fluent in the dominant language or those with disabilities all feel that they are valuable members of the group. Is cultural diversity reflected in and through all the activities? As Duffy (1998:29) notes:

> Creative experiences and imaginative play offer children the opportunity to explore lifestyles outside their immediate family and to gain an insight into the lives of others. The aim is to increase children's understanding by showing images that reflect the real life experiences of families from a variety of cultures... The experiences children have in their homes and communities will affect their uptake of the creative and imaginative experiences we offer.

As we have seen, storytelling sessions are successful when children actively participate. To make this happen they have to feel secure – to feel that they won't be put down, teased or criticised. Similarly, if children's efforts at the activities are appreciated, especially when these are idiosyncratic, their urge to create is likely to be fostered.

By closely observing the children in our group and getting to know them as individuals with their own needs, personalities and aspirations, we are more able to intervene at appropriate times and in ways that sensitively support and extend their creativity, deepen and consolidate their learning and help them develop new skills and knowledge. Most children respond to non-verbal reassurance, for example, being given an encouraging smile or a light touch on the shoulder. By offering help when asked, valuing their input and praising them when they have completed all or part of a task, we acknowledge children's achievements. But children need to feel their efforts are worthy of praise – given too freely, praise can become meaningless.

We could be totally unaware of how certain of our responses to children actually affect them – as this cautionary tale reported by Duffy (1998:101) illustrates:

Shayma, age 5, was working in the graphics area, engrossed in her drawing. When she finished, she came over to me, holding her drawing behind her.

Shayma: I want to show you something.

Me: Oh, let me see, show me.

Shayma: But only if you promise not to ask me to tell you about it.

Me: What do you mean?

Shayma: Every time I show you something you say, 'Oh it's lovely, do tell me about it!' Sometimes I just want to show you my drawings, not tell you about them, sometimes they're for looking at.

During Persona Doll storytelling sessions, the children's identification and bonding with the Dolls usually releases a free flow of feelings, opinions, creativity and imagination. In our role as facilitators we empower children to express this flow but we also direct and control the session. At other times of the day we ensure that children are free to choose from a wide variety of stimulating, imaginative, creative and child directed activities that offer them fresh perspectives and problems to solve.

Open-ended, collaborative and experiential learning opportunities can heighten children's concepts of fairness and empower them to challenge discrimination actively. They can talk about what they think with practitioners who support and guide them without restricting their capacity to contribute ideas. There are plenty of opportunities for children to explore their different priorities and concerns. Trying to see things from the children's perspective enables us to welcome new meanings and ideas. It is fascinating to watch how a child takes up an idea and transforms it in her/his own individual way.

We hope to provide a range of activities to meet the needs of each child but our stereotypical thinking may restrict some children's access to them. For example, we may believe that children from Muslim families are forbidden to depict the human form, but for many in the faith this restriction applies only in mosques. Our own cultural background and mind-set could affect the way we view and understand children's work – as Kate Pahl (1999:76) discovered when observing a group of children making western-style princesses:

> I couldn't see why Abdul had resisted the usual pattern of princesses bedecked with jewels. His version is an elongated figure covered with pieces of cut up paper. ... Abdul has covered the face of his princess with one piece of paper, and then placed more pieces over the entire body, which – beneath the covering – has been coloured in bright, attractive colours. The impression is of a person who is very attractive, brightly coloured and tall, with a small head, who is then concealed. I did not realise the significance of this until later.

It was not until Pahl met Abdul's mother in the playground that she understood why Abdul's representation of a princess was so different from the other children's and why after making something so beautiful and colourful, he had covered it up. His mother was completely veiled. The family was from Somalia. So for Abdul a princess was a tall woman who wore colourful clothes beneath a chador. His version incorporated his own experience. Continuous consultation with parents and other members of the community could mean that our interpretation of children's work has more chance of being culturally sensitive and inclusive.

We may believe that hugely creative and imaginative ability is innate in children from particular groups. Duffy (1998:28) cautions against this conclusion:

> Some groups of Chinese children have highly developed drawing skills at an early age due to the value placed on and early instruction in these skills by the communities in which they live.
>
> Boys often appear to be better than girls at creating three-dimensional representations with construction materials. While this may be partly the result of innate differences, most of the difference is due to the greater encouragement boys receive.

Creative and imaginative activities encourage and enable children to use all their senses, even those which might be impaired. One particularly sensitive key worker was able to expand a little boy's experiences and boost his confidence and self-esteem:

> Anderson, aged 4 years 6 months, was visually impaired. His key worker observed his reluctance to engage in forms of representation which involved fine detail and confined locations, such as drawing while seated at a table. She responded by rearranging the outside space to include large sheets of paper attached to the wall for painting and drawing. Anderson responded with enthusiasm. He concentrated for long periods and returned to his drawings to refine and develop the images. The opportunity to work on a large scale enabled him to make full use of his available sight and the more spacious surroundings allowed him to move without fear of bumping into a person or object. By assessing Anderson's particular needs and altering the way in which

he had access to drawing experiences his key worker helped him to engage in an aspect of creative expression he had previously been denied. Duffy (1998:31)

Extending learning

Developmentally appropriate activities based, for example, on a story or a subject discussed in a story enable us to assess and expand children's understanding, awareness, knowledge, skills and attitudes.

Teaching aim	Scaffolding process
To increase children's vocabulary for talking about different hair texture, such as silky, springy, smooth, crinkly, bristly, curly, straight, spiky.	Hairdressing activity in which children are washing, brushing, drying and combing the dolls' hair that represent children from a variety of ethnic backgrounds.
Shaping their understandings of hair texture.	Giving verbal feedback as children comment on the hair texture, which affirms, negates, recasts, models or hints at what has been said or should be said to be accurate.
Reinforcing a child's proposition that the hair being brushed is very springy.	Restating or expanding what the child has said. For example, 'Yes, I can see that it's hard to brush the doll's lovely curly hair because it's so springy'.
Maintaining joint attention and involvement between child and adult about the different hair textures the child is experiencing and the implements being used to care for the doll's hair	Requesting clarification of what the child has said, reflecting on what has been said or done or asking the child questions. For example, 'Do you think that it might be easier to care for the doll's springy hair using an 'Afro' comb?'
Linking thought and actions by using language to describe them.	Commenting on the present, on what the child or the adult remembers about the situation, or on what the adult thinks about what is happening, and comparing and contrasting thoughts and actions. For example, 'It's hard to make a pony-tail when the doll's hair is so shiny and slippery. Asking Patrick to open the scrunchy for you while you hold the hair together seems to have worked'.
Extending understandings beyond the current situation. We can talk with the children about scientific explanations for differences in hair texture – hair shape determines hair texture, and melanin its colour.	Asking closed and open questions, modelling new understandings, expanding what is said by the child, talking about the implications of what is said, and comparing and contrasting thoughts and actions. For example, we could encourage children to make a chart of the different hair colours in the group. They can talk about whose hair has more melanin.

In chapter seven we noted how we scaffold their learning to extend their level of understanding. The creative opportunities we provide build on what children already know and enable them to gain greater competence through describing, explaining and justifying their thinking. By questioning, prompting, praising, supporting and modelling we can reinforce anti-discriminatory attitudes before as well as after a particular Persona Doll story has been told. In this way we can assess the impact of the story. The following activity adapted from MacNaughton and Williams (1998:275) could be introduced before and after telling a story that highlights a Doll's feelings about its hair. By observing their behaviour and listening to their interactions we can uncover the children's attitudes and knowledge and monitor any changes.

While they are involved in a group activity, children tend to be very interested in what the other members of the group are doing. They watch and learn from one another and comment freely on each other's efforts. By encouraging them to work collaboratively in this way we help to shift the emphasis away from individual competitive attitudes towards active co-operation and away from adults' power and authority to children taking responsibility for their own learning.

We develop topics in a variety of ways through, for instance, discussion, art and craft activities, music, books and displays. The voices of the more articulate and self-assured should not be allowed to drown the less assertive children in the group. Girls often tend to avoid challenging each other, defer to other people's ideas and offer encouragement and support for other speakers in the group, whereas the boys are likely to talk and interrupt more and be more aggressive.

Some refugee children may not have the confidence to participate in activities because they have had little opportunity to play, develop social skills or be creative. They need encouragement and support so they can learn the skills they need and feel safe enough to express their emotions – non-verbal activities are especially helpful. Food, such as pasta, is frequently used in art and craft activities. Parents who are living in poverty and refugees who have come from countries where food is scarce are likely – and justifiably so – to be shocked and offended.

Activities to reinforce and build on Persona Doll stories

Through these activities we hope that children will express their feelings and ideas, develop their ability to empathise with the feelings of others, gain a sense of achievement and enjoy being a valued member of a group.

We know that with young children it is the process not the end product that is of primary importance. Here are a few ideas to get you started – I hope that not all will be familiar. And as Whitehead (1990:177) reminds us:

> It is not the actual things that bridge the home-school gap and make for emotional security, it is what children are doing with and through them that enables the children to feel 'at home' in the world and culture of school and make their own significant contributions to it.

Similarities and differences

Select three children to stand in the middle of the circle. The others find all the things the three have in common and then all the ways in which they differ. Repeat until all the children who want to be in the middle have had a turn.

Provide a variety of objects for children to sort according to their own criteria – e.g. colour, size, shape – and discuss their similarities and differences.

Build up a collection of tights in as many shades as possible so that every child will find at least one that matches her/his skin colour. They'll probably enjoy finding the appropriate pair and putting them on their arms. If practitioners join in they can draw attention to variations in the skin tones of their arms and hands, compare the similarities and differences between the colour of their skin and everyone else's, and encourage the children to do the same. The children could be asked why they think some of them have darker or lighter skins. Children from mixed parentage families and those that are adopted may have different colour skin from their parent(s).

To be on the safe side it might be a good idea to check what adoptive parents have told their children about their adoption – they might have said nothing about it.

Myself

A child's sense of self is closely linked to her/his name. Name clapping is a good way to help children learn each other's names and pronounce them correctly. At circle time, clap a slow rhythm and when the children are all clapping in time with you, go round the circle saying each child's name in rhythm. For example, Ha-tice, Jo, Su-nit-a, Than-da-na-ni, Ann-a-bell. Continue clapping and say your name and call out the name of one of the children who then repeats her/his name and calls out the name of somebody else and so on. Or each child's name could be chanted while beating out the rhythm on a drum. Children are encouraged to listen to and respond to the differences and similarities.

Provide mirrors and strong glue, a range of skin colour crayons, materials of different sizes, shapes, colours and textures for clothes and suggest that the children make pictures of themselves and then 'dress' them. This activity provides a good opportunity to talk about similarities and differences, for example, colour of skin, hair and eyes, shapes of eyes, hair textures and hairstyles.

Encourage the children to contribute a page or more to a group book, or to make their own books. Ask them to bring in photographs of themselves and their families and pictures from magazines to use with their own drawings to illustrate the book. Including members of their family creates opportunities to talk about them and what they do inside and outside the home – this helps highlight, for example, different family structures, practices and sex roles. Add sentences dictated by the children, writing down their exact words because this promotes their confidence in using both the written and spoken word. Those who can write the sentences themselves in English and those who write in languages other than English should be encouraged to do so.

Older children could be invited to write about and illustrate the things they would like other people to know about them. It is up to them to decide what they want to include, for example, the food they like to eat, the games they like to play, the things they can do and the things they can't, the things that make them happy, sad, angry. Provide sheets of sugar paper and a wide range of materials for them to decorate and illustrate their work.

Making books or pictures about their favourite Persona Doll can deepen children's bonding with it and reinforce the messages of the stories about the Doll.

Moving about

Encourage the children to talk about their experiences of moving from nursery or playgroup to school; moving house; moving to another town, from one part of the country to another, from one country to another. By asking appropriate questions we can encourage children to express the positive and negative emotions that were aroused. Be particularly sensitive to any refugee children in the group for whom moving might have been traumatic.

Movement to music is used to try and ensure that children develop constructive, open and sensitive attitudes towards their own bodies and those of others and gives them opportunities to move and use their bodies in various ways – particularly helpful for children with physical impairments. Children with hearing difficulties benefit from rhythmic movement and vibrations.

Talk about the different ways people move their bodies, like walking, running, crawling, waving, nodding, stamping. Motivate them to move in various ways to music from a range of cultures. For example, to move just their feet; just their fingers; their head; and then their whole body without standing up.

Children can express feelings through movement. One way is to use the corners of the room for different feelings and put up signs or draw pictures to illustrate each feeling. When asked 'how do you feel when somebody ...? the children run to the corner with the sign that best describes their feeling. Or the practitioner can name a feeling and ask the children to move around the room acting it out – and then to move in a way that shows an opposite feeling.

Encourage the children to talk about all the different forms of transport that help people move from place to place. Then suggest they draw or make models of some of them – ensure that trailers and wheelchairs are included.

Ways of communicating

Ask the children to tell you all the different ways in which we can communicate without speaking. For example, wave hello or good-bye, using their hands to ask someone to stop or to be quiet. Make different faces and ask them to guess what you're feeling and then you guess their expressions. The next step is to get them to move as if they were feeling excited, angry, scared, worried, happy, surprised.

Sing the song, *If you're happy and you know it* and then change the words to fit other emotions like: if you're sorry/angry/merry/dis-appointed/surprised, and add appropriate actions.

Invite a parent or someone from the community who can tell the children about sign language and teach them a few signs.

Invite parents who are able to speak languages other than the dominant language to teach the children a few phrases or a short song. Acknowledge the ability of children who are able to speak two or more languages.

Ask parents and children to bring in newspapers, carrier bags, maga-zines, anything with writing on it – try to include Braille. Focusing on a variety of scripts raises everyone's awareness. Involve the chil-dren in setting up a display with some of this material (perhaps on an Interest Table) and encourage them to look at and talk about the differences and similarities between the scripts. Then give them large sheets of paper, glue and the remainder of the material, to make collages. Have a display of books in a range of languages, including Signing, Braille and dual text books.

From children's reactions to a wide-ranging collection of photo-graphs we can uncover their positive and negative feelings towards children and adults different from themselves. Their reactions can then be incorporated into Persona Doll stories.

Books like Kathryn Cave's *Something Else* provide opportunities to discuss diversity and help children empathise with the characters who are treated unfairly and can also uncover any stereotypical attitudes and negative beliefs they have picked up. They can be asked questions like:

- What part of the story did you like best? Why?

- Was there any part of the story you didn't like? Why?

- What do you like (not like) about the way the story ends?

- What do you like (not like) about the illustrations?

- How did the story make you feel?

Children can also be the storytellers. At circle time, start telling a story and when you ring a little bell one of the children takes over the story. When that person rings the bell, it will be the turn of someone else. We could begin with a Persona Doll story the children have heard before. It would be interesting to see how closely the children stick to the original story – how much they remember and which part particularly impressed them.

Making story boxes can be fun and gives children opportunities to create a range of 'small worlds', for instance, under the sea, at home, on a farm, in the park. A variety of textured and coloured pieces of paper, card, wool, fabrics, twigs, shells, pebbles and paints, crayons and felt pens can help to trigger children's imaginations.

Helen Bromley (2000) suggests giving each child a shoebox and a collection of small toys and objects that they can use to create stories to tell to their friends. Alternatively, a box can be used by a group of children to start a story and the plot and ending is then developed by individual children, pairs or small groups. The whole group could contribute to the creation of a complete story. Older children could write up and illustrate their stories and younger children could be encouraged to record them on a tape recorder.

Our sensitive support can ensure that children take turns, share the items in the box and listen to each other's ideas. These are the skills we encourage during Persona Doll storytelling sessions and which support the development of the Early Learning Goals. By being interested in the children's stories and their storytelling and carefully observing them we can build our relationship with each child and gain valuable insights into their interests, knowledge, attitudes and ideas.

Story sacks containing a picture book with soft toys representing the main characters, together with props and scenery, help to bring books to life. The books we choose can reinforce the ideas, feelings and attitudes raised during Persona Doll storytelling sessions. Parents can be involved in making the sacks and enjoy sharing books with their children.

Exploring feelings

Children select two A5 sheets of paper they think most closely match the colour of their skin. Ask them to draw a happy face on one piece of paper, a sad face on the other and paste a spatula onto the back of each. They are encouraged to show each other happy and sad expressions and talk about their drawings while they work. Once they have completed this task they sit in a circle with a practitioner. They practice responding to her/his shout of happy or sad face by holding up the appropriate one. She/he then tells them that she/he is going to ask them some questions and they must answer by holding up the face that describes how they feel.

Questions like:

How do you feel when somebody smiles at you?
How do you feel if somebody shouts at you?
How do you feel when somebody gives you a present?
How do you feel when somebody tells you that they like you?
How do you feel when somebody calls you names?
How do you feel when somebody gives you a hug?

The children then take turns asking the questions and the adult joins in with her/his own happy and sad face pictures. This activity can be extended by having the children make a range of faces showing various emotions and using these to respond to an extended range of questions and to talk about their choices.

Act or mime a range of emotions and ask the children to guess what you are feeling. Children then volunteer to act out feelings for the other children to guess. This could lead to discussing what makes them happy, sad, grumpy etc and how they express their feelings. The group could be asked who they talk to when they need help to sort things out.

Music can be used to encourage children to express their feelings. Play different pieces of music and ask the children to say how each one makes them feel. Providing mood music while children are painting can affect what and how they paint. With adult encouragement some children may be willing to talk about how it makes them feel. On another occasion introduce two contrasting pieces and gradually introduce more, ensuring that the selection includes music from a range of cultures.

Many children enjoy listening to poems that express feelings they can identify with, like this one. With encouragement they might make up their own.

ME, MYSELF

I'm sitting on the doorstep and I'm eating bread and jam
And I aren't crying really though I 'specs you think I am.

I can hear the children playing
but they say they don't want me
'Cause my legs are rather little
and I run so slow you see.

So I'm sitting on the doorstep and I'm eating bread and jam
And I aren't crying really though I 'specs you think I am.

Source unknown

Drama and role-playing

Basing drama and role-playing on Persona Doll stories highlights diversity, focuses on fair and unfair situations and enables children to explore issues and express their feelings in a safe environment. In the process they can find out what it feels like to be in someone else's shoes. Dramatising stories and encouraging the children to act out alternative story lines or endings to familiar stories can stimulate lively discussion, develop critical awareness and foster empathy.

If a video-camera is available, events, activities and interactions in the setting can be recorded and shown to the children. This has been found to help them see how they relate to one another and encourage them to respond to unfair situations. They will probably enjoy seeing themselves 'on telly' so be sure that all the children are filmed.

Interest tables

These can be set up to reflect particular themes or topics raised during storytelling sessions and the children invited to bring in relevant items from home to encourage feelings of belonging and the sharing of lifestyles, experiences and interests. Children from refugee families, especially those recently arrived in Britain, could feel isolated, ashamed and embarrassed if they have little to bring in. This also applies to children from families who are living in poverty.

If the children in the group are all monolingual and if one or more of the Dolls is bilingual then include books written in the languages the children and the Doll(s) 'speak' – children can be asked to bring some from home.

The more we involve parents the more authentic and accessible our displays are likely to be but we always need to ascertain how they feel about sharing particular aspects of their family and cultural background. Most will probably be happy to but some may not, and we have to respect their feelings.

If items are offered that we think are likely to promote racist, sexist or other negative stereotypes, we would have to explain to the children and their parents why they are unacceptable. This would need to be done with great care and sensitivity. Practitioners who feel comfortable about bringing items from their own homes and communities could use them with the children to trigger discussion and comments and could heighten the children's interest in the display and spark their curiosity.

We need to ensure that children with physical impairments are able to touch and explore everything on the table. Sense tables and items that demonstrate the special abilities of sight and hearing-impaired children can send positive messages to all the children. For example, the ability of a sight-impaired child to identify objects in a 'feely' box or bag correctly is likely to impress the other children.

Evaluating through documentation

Art and craft activities provide us with a tool for monitoring and evaluating the degree to which the Dolls and their stories are influencing children's attitudes and beliefs. People who have seen the Reggio Emilia approach of documenting and displaying children's project work seem convinced that it is a useful way to record this process. Documenting each child's work provides a window on what they are learning and records any changes in their thinking and attitudes. Video-tape recordings of children's interactions, observations and photographic evidence are woven together with samples of work to provide an on-going profile of each child's learning. These are shared, discussed and interpreted at daily staff team meetings. Records of the children's learning stay on the walls throughout the time that they are in the setting – an effective way to show progression. Documentation also provides opportunities for practitioners to learn and to increase communication and collaboration with parents and it enables children to revisit their work, construct and reconstruct their feelings and ideas.

Recording changes in children's thinking and attitudes in this way involves checking whether bias is influencing our decisions about what to document and how to interpret what we document – not just what interests or is attractive to us.

- Is the work of every child being valued?

- Do activities challenge stereotypical thinking and promote collaboration and co-operation?

During Persona Doll storytelling and creative activity sessions, children are not simply passive recipients of information. They are actively engaged in questioning, reflecting and communicating. By providing a stimulating environment with plenty of collaborative and co-operative learning experiences, we lay the foundation for children to become creative rather than dependent learners. We are putting this ancient Chinese Proverb into practice:

I hear and I forget
I see and I remember
I do and I understand.

We are powerful people

In the introduction to this book I identified the aim as being to develop children's ability to empathise with the Dolls, to care about them, to recognise the ways in which they are similar to and different from themselves and to appreciate the hurt that prejudiced attitudes and discriminatory behaviour can cause. If we use Persona Dolls appropriately we can encourage children to respond to others with respect and sensitivity. We can build on their sense of identity, their self-esteem and their confidence. We can empower them to stand up when they experience or witness discrimination. A tall order but the Dolls are well able to meet the challenge! We are too – but we need constantly to reflect on our own attitudes and practices because, as Louise Derman-Sparks says (cited in Brown 1998:xi)

> All social change takes commitment, persistence, courage and a vision of the future we want. I cannot imagine a more exciting and satisfying way of being an early years educator than joining in the work of creating a more caring and just world for all children.

Let us strive to create the kind of society described by Aung San Suu Kyl, the Burmese political leader at the Non-Government Organisations Forum on Women in 1995 in China: *'where men are truly confident of their own worth, women are not merely tolerated but valued'*. And in the words of Sarah Grimke, a US abolitionist and feminist *'I ask no favours for my sex. All I ask is that [men] take their feet from off our necks.'* She was born in 1792 and died in1873!! As Fidel Castro said: 'The road is long and patience is needed'.

10

Resourcing for change

Good resources present children with positive images of themselves and their families. They fire children's imaginations, stimulate their curiosity about the people and the world around them, extend their general knowledge about and understanding of diversity and are a source of pleasure and delight. But good resources will not, by themselves, change children's attitudes and behaviour. The crucial factor is how we present them, and how we encourage children to use them.

We can use books that confront discriminatory issues sensitively and appropriately to enable young children to learn about the world, share their own cultural traditions and learn about others, and to recognise and challenge stereotypes. Doing so is particularly important for children whose communities or countries of origin or whose abilities are traditionally viewed negatively, and for children who have absorbed and express prevailing negative views. Children can be encouraged to adopt a critical approach to text and illustrations and to notice and comment when they portray characters inappropriately, negatively or stereotypically.

It is heartening to come across books in which the leading characters are strong, thoughtful girls and women. In some, sexist stereotypes are challenged and in others the stories are warm and tender. Those that portray housewives and mothers as strong, independent, warm and loving women can stimulate discussion about children's mothers, aunts and grandmothers. Sue Adler (1993:113) calls such books feminist and explains that: *'Feminism is not only concerned with the struggle for political and economic change but also with valuing women's experience, with notions (however idealistic) of sisterhood, and therefore with challenges to patriarchy'.*

Working from an anti-discriminatory perspective requires that we select the books we offer children carefully. We need to ensure that we include books written in a range of languages, or in two languages, to support the home languages of the bilingual children in the group and to develop all the children's interest in and knowledge about languages other than their own.

Some books that are anti-sexist, antiracist or both or which include positive images of disabled people and of men doing domestic chores, still perpetuate the idea that all families consist of a mother, a father and their children, usually a boy and a girl. Although there are a growing number of books that feature different ways of living in a family there is still a need for practitioners to make their own.

Anti-discriminatory books support and, in many cases, develop the issues that Persona Doll stories address. The books suggested here represent only a cross-section of those that broaden children's knowledge and understanding, encourage them to empathise, think critically and build on their sense of fairness and justice. Many are published outside the UK and are not available in local bookshops or libraries but you should be able to order them from suppliers like those on pages 190-193. Some of these suppliers exist today because in the 1970s and 1980s there were so few books on the market that reflected their own families or the wider community. For instance, Letterbox Library was started by two mothers who wanted children to have the opportunity to enjoy books celebrating diversity. Thanks to publishers like Tamarind, Mantra, Barefoot Books and Milet, a growing number are being written and produced in Britain.

Positive images of Black children and their families

Amazing Grace by Mary Hoffmann is available in a range of languages for 5 to 10 year olds. Her grandmother tells her she can be whatever she wants to be. In the sequel, *Grace and Family*, she visits her father in the Gambia and learns that families are what you make them.

A is for Africa by Ifeoma Onyefulu, *C is for China* by Sungwan So and *I is for India* by Prodeepta Das are remarkable alphabet books, bringing the peoples of Africa, China and India to life through words and photos.

Billie and Belle by Sarah Garland, for 4 to 8 year olds, is about the arrival of a new baby into a mixed parentage family.

Billy the Great by Rosa Guy is a sympathetically told story for the over 7s in which children's friendships override parental prejudices.

Celebrations by Chris Deshpande, for 5 to 11 year olds, includes simply explained ideas for craft activities based on festivals and traditions around the world.

Cherish Me by Joyce Carol Thomas, for 1 to 3 year olds, is a beautiful poem with lively pictures that portray a little girl's sense of her own identity.

Chicken Sunday by Patricia Polacco, for 6 to 11 year olds, tells the story of a friendship between a Russian-Jewish child in the USA, her African-American friends and their grandma.

Emeka's Gift, also by Ifeoma Onyefulu, is an original counting book in which Emeka sees all kinds of fascinating people and things on his way to visit his grandmother.

I Love My Hair by Natasha Anastasia Turpley, for 4 to 9 year olds, focuses on the versatility of African hair.

Jamaica and Brianna by Juanitta Havill, for 4 to 7 year olds, is a beautifully observed story and a welcome addition to: *Jamaica Tag-Along* and *Jamaica's Find*.

Mai-Li's Surprise by Marjorie Jackson, for 3 to 8 year olds, describes a girl and her brother making a kite. Key words are shown in Chinese characters.

Mama Elizabethi by Stephanie Stuve-Bodeen, for 4 to 8 year olds, is a loving family story with stunning illustrations.

My Hair is Beautiful Because it's Mine and *My Skin is Brown* by Paula deJoie are board books celebrating the diversity of Black hair and skin tones.

My Painted House, My Friendly Chicken And Me by Maya Angelou, for 5 to 8 year olds, introduces Thandi and her family and friends in a Ndebele village in South Africa.

Through my Window, Wait and See and *In a Minute* by Tony Bradman and Eileen Browne are for 3 to 7 year olds. In the first, Joe is ill and stays home with her White dad while her Black mum goes to work. In the second, Joe and mum go shopping, and in the third, they go to the park.

Shades of Black by Sandra Pinkney is an affirmative book for nursery age upwards.

W is for World by Kathryn Cave and *Wake Up World* are alphabet books which take 4 to 8-year-olds on a fascinating journey. Along the way they meet children working and playing, enjoying food and music and getting to know their world.

Positive images of Gypsy/Traveller children and their families

There are few books for the under 8s featuring Gypsies/Travellers on sale in bookshops – some listed here are out of print but Traveller Education Centres are likely to have copies you can borrow. In addition many Centres produce books of stories written by Traveller children or their parents, which provide interesting insights into their lives. A complete list of Traveller Education Services can be obtained from the National Association of Teachers of Travellers. Its address and the names and addresses of some other centres appear on page 194-195.

Snowy by Berlie Doherty, for 4-8 year olds, published by Picture Lions is available in bookshops and tells the story of Rachel who lives in a narrow boat. She loves living on a boat but most of all she loves their horse, Snowy, who pulls it.

Gypsy Family by Mary Waterson, for 4-8 year olds, is part of A&C Black's Strands series. It is a simple and realistic portrayal of a travelling family describing the way they live, the different places they travel to and some of their reasons for moving.

Melissa's Story by Sandy Madden, published by the Avon Consortium Traveller Education Service, is about a girl in a Traveller family who finds a lost foal.

Stone Soup by Beryl Williams, published by the Oxfordshire Advisory Service for the Education of Travellers, is a traditional tale about a wise old Traveller who comes into a village with his traditional trailer and makes stone soup.

Two books in the Nipper series by Geraldine Kaye for Infants and Juniors portray particular events and frustrations in Traveller life:

Christmas is a Baby is about a cold Christmas when mum is about to have a baby. Unfortunately the family are also having trouble in finding somewhere to stop.

In *Pegs and Flow*, mum shows the children how she used to make pegs and flowers from wood.

Two books produced by the Norfolk Traveller Education Service are:

Shaun's Wellies, an illustrated interactive book for the early years about his search for his wellies on the Traveller site where he lives.

A Family Business is about Scott, who takes an active part in helping with the family's scrapping business. It is illustrated with photographs.

Two books from the Haringey Traveller Education Service:

Just Like You (1999) is a photographic book showing Traveller children and their families at home and school. It gives a clear message about the similarities and differences between Traveller lifestyles and those of the settled community

Stories from Travelling Children includes stories written and illustrated by Traveller children ranging in age from 6 to 14. They provide informative, interesting personal insights into the Traveller way of life.

Challenging sexism and promoting feminism

ABC ... I can be by Verna Wilkins, for 3 to 8 year olds, aims to expand their horizons, raise their aspirations and provide positive role models.

A Chair for my Mother by Vera B Williams is for 5 to 8 year olds. After a fire destroys their home, Rosa, her mother and grandmother save to buy a chair they can all enjoy.

Grandma and Me by Caroline Boston Weatherford, for 2 to 4 year olds, is a warm and loving story that describes in rhyme the fun shared by a little girl and her grandmother.

I Look Like a Girl by Sheila Hamanaka, for 3 to 7 year olds, celebrates girlhood and imagination with lyrical text and exuberant illustrations.

I Want to Be by Thylias Moss, for 4 to 7 year olds, describes all the things a young girl would like to be.

Jump by Michelle Magorian, for 3 to 8 year olds is about overcoming sexist stereotyping. As he watches his sister's ballet class, Steven decides that he too wants to dance.

My Mum Is So Unusual by Iris Lowen, gives a daughter's view of her funny, sometimes cross and scared but always loving, mum. A positive portrayal of a single parent family.

Mum Goes to Work by Libby Gleeson, for 3 to 6 year olds, is unusual because working mothers rarely feature in children's books. Moments from their mother's working days are echoed in the children's activities at their day centre.

Mum Can Fix It by Verna Wilkins is for 4 to 8 year olds. In seven simple steps Mum shows the children how to change the wheel on the car without waiting for help to arrive.

Only Molly by Cally Poplack, for 5 to 8 year olds, describes the adventures of an independent little girl and her mother – from wet knickers to that special dress.

Pass it Polly by Sarah Garland, for 5 to 8 year olds, is an anti-sexist story about Polly and her friends learning to play football so they can play in a match.

The Princess who Danced with Cranes by Annette Lebox is for 6 to 10 year olds. The beautiful land is almost destroyed until brave Princess Vivian saves it.

The Roses Sing on New Snow by Paul Yee, for 4 to 8 year olds, is a Chinese tale in which a girl's wisdom and skill are rewarded.

This is our House by Michael Rosen is for 3 to 7 year olds. George says, This house isn't for girls but his friends find a way to include and share equally.

Toby's Doll's House by Ragnhild Scannell and Adrian Reynolds is for 4 to 8 year olds. Toby wants a doll's house but his family keep giving him toys they think are right for him.

What is a Girl? What is a Boy? by Stephanie Waxman, for 4 to 7 year olds, helps children discover their sexual identities.

Zora Hurston and the Chinaberry Tree by William Miller for the over 4s is an inspiring, moving book based on Zora's childhood. Her mother teaches her to believe in herself, to fight sexism and to hold on to the stories of her people.

Positive images of children and adults with disabilities

Are We There Yet? by Verna Wilkins, for 3 to 7 year olds, describes the rides and surprises of a family day out in a theme park with a wheelchair-user dad.

Aria by Peter Ebling and Sophy Williams, for 4 to 8 year olds, is about Aria, whose imitation of the bird calls of the rain forest help her forget that she cannot speak.

Big Brother Dustin by Alden Carter is for 3 to 7 year olds. Nobody can think of a name for the new baby but Dustin, the loving older brother with Down's Syndrome, comes up with the perfect one.

Cleversticks by Derek Brazell is for 4 to 7 year olds. Ling Sung doesn't want to go to school because everybody else is clever at doing the things he can't. He discovers that he can do something that nobody else can.

Dad and Me in the Morning by Patricia Lakin, for 4 to 10 years olds, captures the loving relationship between a hearing-impaired boy and his Dad. Signing, lip reading or just squeezing hands, they share a dawn walk.

Friends at School by Rochelle Burnette, for 3 to 7 year olds, captures the warmth of this integrated classroom as children with different abilities work and play.

I Wonder who Lives Upstairs by Edel Wignell and Leanne Argent is for 3 to 6 year olds. When Sophie visits the new family upstairs she discovers that Hannibal is a hearing dog with an important job to do.

Jessy and the Long-Short Dress by Rachel Anderson is for 6-10 year olds. Jessy, a child with Down's Syndrome, wears a bridesmaid's dress at her teacher's wedding.

Letang's New Friend, Letang and Julie Save the Day and *Trouble for Letang and Julie* are three books for 4 to 7 year olds by Beverley Naidoo about Letang, recently arrived from Botswana and her friend Julie, a wheelchair user.

Listen for the Bus: David's Story by Patricia McMahon, for 5 to 11 year olds, describes a typical day at home and school. David is blind and hearing-impaired.

Lucy's Picture by Nicola Moon is for 3 to 7 year olds. Lucy doesn't want to use the teacher's bright colours to do a painting. With determination and ingenuity she makes a collage especially for her Granddad to see.

Mama Zooms by Jane Cowen-Fletcher, for 3 to 7 year olds, describes a young boy zooming with his mother in her wheelchair.

Monty's Ups and Downs and *Monty's Midnight Snack* by Colin West, for over 5s, are about Monty the dog who wears glasses. Both books could be used to trigger discussion on the attitude to and use of aids.

Mom Can't See Me by Sally Hobart Alexander, for over 5s, is a very positive and moving portrayal of family life from a daughter's point of view.

Name Games by Theresa Breslin, for over 5s, is about Jane who hates her name and decides on something more unusual – with unexpected consequences.

Susan Laughs by Jeanne Willis, for over 6s, is a witty and profound book about disability with whimsical pictures and won the NASEN award for 2000.

Talk to Me by Sue Brearley, for 5 to 8 year olds, shows ways of talking and sharing feelings.

The Boy Who Wouldn't Speak by Steve Barry, tells the story of Owen, who befriends the two giants who have moved into his road. A campaign is launched to make them move away. Only when he needs to defend his two friends does Owen speak.

We can do it! by Laura Dwight, for 5 to 9 year olds, introduces five children who show that disability is not a barrier to friends, enjoyment and activities.

Where's Chimpy? by Berniece Rabe, for 3 to 7 year olds, features Misty, a girl with Down's Syndrome and an infectious sense of humour who loses and finds her toys.

Dealing with a range of issues

These books could be used to extend some of the activities suggested in chapter nine.

All Kinds of People and *All Kinds of Beliefs* by Emma Damon, for 4 to 8 year olds, has flaps to open, questions and a mirror. These books provide a wonderful way for children to explore identity and different faiths.

Facing the Day by Laurel Gugler, for 5+, is a rhyming picture book that follow the moods, highs and lows, challenges and joys of a child through the day.

Farmer Duck by Martin Waddell is for 3 to 7 year olds. A farmer who exploits his animals wakes up one morning to find that they have taken over the running of the farm. The book is available in range of languages and as a big book.

Farmyard Tales: from far and near, retold by Wendy Cooling, for 4 to 7 year olds, includes stories from a number of countries. The illustrations are bright and bold.

For every child by Caroline Castle highlights fourteen of the UN Convention's Rights of the Child in child-friendly language and is beautifully illustrated.

Frederick Douglas by William Miller, for 6+, describes his early life as a plantation slave.

Great Women in the Struggle edited by Toyomi Igus, for 7 to 12 year olds, profiles eighty historical and contemporary Black women.

Jasha and Jamil Went Down the Hill by Virginia Kroll, for 5+, is an African rendering of Mother Goose verses that preserves all the fun of the originals while matching them to a modern treasury of rhyme and rhythm.

Martha's Friends by Emma Damon is a lift-the-flap story for 4 to 8 year olds. Martha is shy and lonely but, by standing up to a bully, she discovers pride in the differences that make us all unique.

My Two Uncles by Judith Vigna is for children of 7 upwards. Plans for a family party expose the reluctance of Elly's grandfather to accept a gay relationship in the family. A story of prejudice overcome, told in Elly's own words.

One day we had to run is for 7 to 12 year olds. Refugee children from Somalia, Sudan and Ethiopia tell their stories through words and paintings.

One Grain of Rice by Demi, for 6 to 12 year olds, describes how clever Rani outwits the stingy Raja and provides the starving villagers with rice in abundance by her knowledge of multiplication.

Sami and the Time of Troubles by Florence Parry Heide and Judith Heide Gilliland, for 7 to 10 year olds, provides a lyrical, haunting picture of a Lebanese child caught up in the horrors of war. A tribute to human courage and hope – a powerful anti-war book.

Since Dad Left by Caroline Binch, for 5 to 9 year olds, is about a little boy's anger at his parents separation. Stunning pictures show how he comes to enjoy sharing the pleasures of his dad's alternative lifestyle, and capture his conflicting emotions.

Someone I like compiled by Judith Nicholls, for 4+, includes poems from many cultures exploring human relationships

Something Else by Kathryn Cave, is for 5 to 9 year olds. Children will empathise with Something Else in his desperate attempts to fit in and how he finds a friend. Winner of the 1997 UNESCO prize for promoting tolerance.

The Lotus Seed by Sherry Garland, for 7 upwards, is a thought-provoking story about a Vietnamese woman's memories of emperors, wars and struggle. Throughout her life she treasures a lotus seed, symbol of life and hope.

Where has Daddy Gone? by Trudi Osman, for 4-9 year olds, sensitively and positively describes a child's pain when parents split up.

Young Harriet Tubman by Anne Benjamin is for 5 to 8 year olds. Harriet emerged from the hardships of being a slave to lead her people to freedom.

Young Martin Luther King by Joanne Mattern, for 5 to 8 year olds, describes his early life clearly and simply.

Videos and CD-Roms

ALTOGETHER BETTER consists of a booklet and video that clearly explain why it is important to educate children with disabilities in mainstream schools. It discusses the issues facing teachers who want to include children with disabilities naturally in their school. From Comic Relief Education, Unit 2 Drywall Estate Castle Road Sittingbourne ME10 3RL.

A WORLD OF DIFFERENCE is an entertaining and thought provoking animated video that imaginatively raises issues around effective school practices. From Leeds Animation Workshop, 45 Bayswater Row Leeds LS8 5LF. Tel: 0113 248 4997.

COMBATING DISCRIMINATION: Persona Dolls In Action highlights the variety of ways in which Persona Dolls can be used to develop empathy and challenge inequality. The video is designed to empower, inspire and inform advisers, lecturers, in-service trainers, practitioners and students and through the activities in the accompanying workbook further to develop the issues raised in the video. From Persona Dolls Training 51 Granville Road London N12 0JH. Tel: 020 8446 7056 and from EYTARN PO Box 28 Wallasey CH45 9NP. Tel: 0151 639 1778. Available from July 2001.

DON'T SUFFER IN SILENCE is a new anti-bullying pack for schools which stresses the importance of taking parents seriously when they complain that their children are being bullied. It shows the need for the whole school to be involved if an anti-bullying policy is to succeed. Television celebrities are featured. From DfEE Publications, Sanctuary Building, Great Smith Street London SW1P. Tel: 0845 602 2260.

EDUCATING THE WHOLE CHILD is based on an holistic approach proposing that the silencing and the invisibility of children's cultural, racial and social identity lies at the heart of race, gender and class inequalities. Centre for Children's Rights, 356 Holloway Road London N7 6PA. Tel 020 7700 8127.

HOMEBEATS: struggles for racial justice is anti-racist and interactive education at its best. The depth of information and comprehensive coverage make this CD-ROM a must for every library and those involved in adult training and education. Produced by the Institute of Race Relations and available from them and from EYTARN PO Box 28 Wallasey CH45 9NP. Tel 0151 639 1778.

NEW EUROPEANS is a video study pack designed to promote discussion on anti-racism in Europe with 15+ students. An innovative approach to teaching about issues of racism and xenophobia is used to capture attention, provide information and influence attitudes. The pack includes two videos and excellent notes that provide an historical backdrop and includes 40 activity pages with questions for discussion that can be photocopied. From EYTARN PO Box 28 Wallasey CH45 9NP. Tel 0151 639 1778.

RESPECT FOR DIVERSITY IN EARLY CHILDHOOD CARE AND EDUCATION is a CD-ROM that can be used for individual study as well as on initial and in-service training. The theoretical framework is based on the work of Louise Derman-Sparks and on experiences in Belgium, France, Ireland and Britain. Users can surf through the recruitment and selection procedures and evaluate how to build a multiethnic team; 'walk' through a daycare centre that values diversity; listen to the experiences of parents in the centre and browse in the library. It contains background texts in original languages and a glossary in Dutch, English and French. From Kent Early Years and Childcare Unit Oakwood House, Oakwood Park, Maidstone ME16 8AE

RESOLVING CONFLICT is a new video containing nine separate units designed for young people from14 years upwards. It poses a number of questions, such as: 'Why does violence begin?' and 'What do you do when things get out of hand?' People speak out about violence and conflict; about losing face; about standing up for themselves and about re-establishing relationships. A workbook accompanies the video. From Team Video Productions, 222 Kensal Road, London W10 5BN.

THROUGH THE GLASS CEILING is an animated fairy story but its theme of equal opportunity at work is firmly set in the real world. The narration on this video by Alan Bennett is brilliant. From Leeds Animation Workshop, 45 Bayswater Row Leeds LS8 5LF. Tel 0113 248 4997.

SUPPLIERS OF BOOKS, TOYS AND EQUIPMENT

Imagine looking in a mirror and not seeing a reflection. That is what it is like for parents and their children who come into settings in which their cultures, communities and way of life are not acknowledged and represented. Resources need to be continually monitored and evaluated to ensure that conscious and unconscious racism, sexism, class, ableism and homophobia are not reinforced and that all children's general knowledge, imagination and self-esteem are fostered.

Toys and other learning materials are not in themselves discriminatory but they reflect the values and attitudes of the society in which they are used. Concern stems from the fact that in Britain children pick up negative messages about themselves and other people. From TV and from many of their toys, children learn that some facial features are more beautiful than others, that straight hair is 'better' than 'kinky' hair, that light skin is 'better' than dark skin and that beautiful people are perfect – they don't have impairments. Boys and girls also learn which toys they are supposed to play with.

Some manufacturers and publishers are producing toys and other learning materials that challenge stereotypes and present positive images of and for all children. We need many more of them and their products need to be far more widely available. At present they tend to be on sale in specialist shops and only rarely in the High Street. Practitioners can order positive resources through catalogues but these are not generally available to parents and the general public. Here are some of the suppliers that counter discrimination and promote respect for a range of lifestyles and cultures.

ACORN PERCUSSION have instruments, to suit all age groups and abilities. Unit 33, Abbey Business Centre, Ingate Place, London SW8 3NS. Tel 020 7720 2243.

ACTION FOR LEISURE and PLANET is an information resource for children, young people and adults with disabilities. c/o Warwickshire College, Moreton Morell Centre, Moreton Morell Warwick CV35 9BL Tel 01926 650 195.

AMS EDUCATIONAL distributes a range of multicultural resources including many produced by the ILEA. Woodside Trading Estate, Low Lane Leeds LS18 5NY. Tel 0113 258 0309.

BANGLADESH CENTRE stocks a range of dolls, toys, books, handicrafts and instruments reflecting the history and culture of Bangladesh. PO Box 21711 London E14 6ST. Tel 020 7537 1199.

BAREFOOT BOOKS publish and market a range of books. 18 Highbury Crescent London N5 1UP. Tel 020 7704 6492 for their catalogue.

BEDFORDSHIRE MULTICULTURAL EDUCATION RESOURCES offers a variety of consultancy and training packages. Emerald Court, Pilgrim House 20 Brickhill Drive Bedford MK41 7PZ. Tel 01234 316 040.

BLACK RIVER BOOKS specialise in cards, books, puzzles and dolls. At 232 Stapleton Road Easton Bristol. Tel 0117 952 1965.

CENTRE FOR YOUNG CHILDREN'S RIGHTS (formerly EQUALITY LEARN-ING CENTRE) is a Save the Children project providing resources and information on race gender, disability and children's rights. 356 Holloway Road London N7 6PA. Tel 020 7700 8127.

CHAMELEON is a book showroom exclusively for the teaching profession. 5 Milnyard Square, Orton Southgate, Peterborough PE2 6GX. Tel 01733 370606.

CHANGS aims to provide good quality Chinese arts and crafts as well as puppets and children's dressing up clothes. 14 Pollards Hill East, London SW16 4UT. Tel 020 8764 8377.

COMMUNITY EDUCATION DEVELOPMENT CENTRE (CEDC) produces a wide range of materials. Lyng Hall, Blackberry Lane Coventry CV2 3JS. Tel 024 7638 660.

COMMUNITY INSIGHT carry a range of books focusing on child development and equality issues as well as children's books. Pembroke Centre, Cheney Manor, Swindon SN2 2PQ. Tel 01793 512 612.

DEVELOPMENT EDUCATION CENTRE produce a wide range of carefully piloted materials. 998 Bristol Road, Selly Oak, Birmingham B29 6LE. Tel 0121 472 3255.

EARLY YEARS TRAINERS ANTI-RACIST NETWORK , EYTARN, has a range of anti-racist resources. PO Box 28 Wallasey CH45 9NP. Tel 0151 639 1778.

EASTSIDE BOOKS aims to increase access to books and reading. 178 White-chapel Road London E1 1BJ. Tel 0171 247 0216.

EAST-WEST EDUCATION markets a variety of authentic Indian clothes for dolls made by disadvantaged young women in Bangalore. 3 Keymer Gardens, Burgess Hill Sussex RH15 0AF. Tel 01444 236 322.

EDU-PLAY has resources for play/therapy, learning difficulties and early learning. Vulcan Business Centre Units H and I Vulcan Road Leicester LE5 3EB. Tel: 0116 262 5827.

ESG LONDON TEACHING AND LEARNING RESOURCES stocks interactive and multi-sensory materials. 4 Manor Lane Terrace London SE13 5QL. Tel 020 8318 1307.

GALT EDUCATIONAL and PRESCHOOL have a range of play equipment. Johnsonbrook Road, Hyde, Cheshire SK14 4QT. Tel 0161 882 5300.

KIDSACTIVE (formerly HAPA) produces information packs, a checklist for accessible play and welcome posters featuring a variety of sign and symbol languages. Fulham Palace, Bishop's Avenue London SW6 6EA. Tel 020 7731 1435.

KIMM-BARRAL-DESIGN supply West African fabrics, percussion instruments, dolls, posters, tapes and clothing. PO Box 2777, Sawbridgeworth, Herts. CM21 9RH. Tel 0850 806 837.

KNOCK ON WOOD supply a comprehensive range of music, instruments, books and recordings. Unit 131 Glasshouses Mill, Harrogate HG3 5QH. Tel 0142 371 2712.

KNOCKABOUTS produce good quality wooden trailers and puzzles as well as templates. 23 Wheatacres Thetford Norfolk IP24 1AQ. Tel 01842 762 560.

LEICESTERSHIRE RESOURCE CENTRE FOR MULTICULTURAL EDUCA-TION (RCME) provides multicultural/antiracist resources, collaborative learning activities and resources to support children learning English as an additional language during the literacy hour. Forest Lodge Education Centre Charnor Road Leicester LE3 6LH. Tel 0116 231 3399.

LETTERBOX LIBRARY provide accurate descriptions in their catalogue of non-sexist and multicultural books for children. 71 Allen Road London N16 8RY. Tel: 020 7226 1633.

MANTRA PUBLISHING produces books, friezes and posters. 5 Alexander Grove London N12 8NU. Tel: 020 8445 5123.

MILET LTD publishes and distributes Turkish and dual language books for children. PO Box 9916 London W14 0GS. Tel 020 7603 5477.

MULTICULTURAL BOOKSHOP has posters, artefacts and videos and resources on Pakistan. Rachid House, Westgate, Bradford BD1 3AA. Tel 0127 473 1908.

THE MULTICULTURAL STUDY CENTRE provides classroom and professional development support on all aspects of equality. 451 High Road London N12 0AS. Tel 020 8359 3995.

NESARNOLD distribute a wide range of play equipment. Novara House, Excelsior Road, Ashby Park, Ashby de la Zouche LE65 1NG. Tel: 01159 452201.

NEWS FROM NOWHERE is a feminist bookshop. 112 Bold Street Liverpool L1. Tel 0151 708 7270.

PAUBLO BOOKS LTD supply books written mainly by Black authors. PO Box 167 Greenford Middx UB6 9YX. Tel 020 8575 6181.

PERSONA DOLL TRAINING carries a range of culturally appropriate tall dolls (30 inches). From 51 Granville Road London N12 0JH. Tel: 020 8446 7056.

PLAYMATTERS (NATIONAL TOY LIBRARIES ASSOCIATION) stock a range of books and toys for children with disabilities. 68 Church Way London NW1 1LT Tel 020 7387 9592.

PLAYGEAR, London Educational Suppliers caters for early years providers and parents of young children. 3 Dennis Parade, Winchmore Hill Road London N14 6AA. Tel 020 8882 4700.

POSITIVE IMAGES offers a set of 12 A4 laminated posters featuring images of young children. 5 Woodcliffe Drive Chislehurst Kent BR7 5NT. Tel 020 7613 0838.

PRE-SCHOOL EDUCATION RESOURCE CENTRE supplies a wide range of play materials. 2-4 Roscoe Street Liverpool L1 2SX. Tel 0151 708 7698.

PRIORITY PLAYSTORE stocks a range of posters and books. Unit G16, Marinners House, Queens Dock, 3 Commercial Centre, Norfolk Street Liverpool L1 0B. Tel 0151 708 7698.

REDE EDUCATIONAL LIMITED produce beautifully made wooden puzzles. 153 Redehall Road, Burstow RH6 9RJ. Tel 01342 717538.

ROY YATES BOOKS specialises in dual-language books for children. Smallfields Cottage, Cox Green, Horsham RH12 3DE. Tel 0140 382 2299.

SOMA BOOKS stocks a wide range of books on South Asia, Africa and the Caribbean and specialise in dual text books for children. 38 Kennington Lane London SE11 4LS. Tel 020 7735 2101.

SOURCE BOOKS specialise in black literature and educational materials. 3 Myrtle Parade, Liverpool 7. Tel 0151 708 5474.

STEP BY STEP is a mail-order company specialising in products for the under-fives. Holgate Street Waterhead Oldham OL4 2JF. Tel 0845 300 1089.

TAMARIND LTD produces and distributes books to challenge ethnic and gender stereotyping. PO Box 52, Northwood Middlesex HA6 1UN. Tel 020 8866 5627.

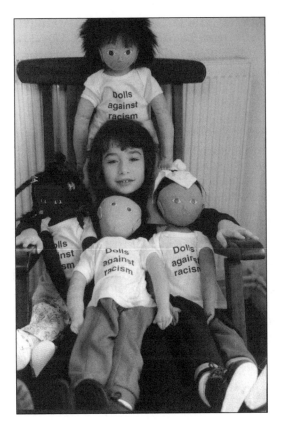

ORGANISATIONS OFFERING GUIDANCE AND SUPPORT

Anti-Racism

ARTEN ANTI-RACIST TEACHER EDUCATION NETWORK c/o Alison Hatt, Flat 5, 19 Hillbury Road, London SW17 8JT.

BLACK CHILDCARE NETWORK 17 Brownhill Road London SE6 2EG.

CENTRE FOR YOUNG CHILDREN'S RIGHTS (EQUALITY LEARNING CENTRE) 356 Holloway Road London N7 6PA. Tel 020 7700 8127.

COMMISSION FOR RACIAL EQUALITY Elliot House, Allington Street London SW1E 5EH. Tel 020 7828 7022.

EYTARN – EARLY YEARS TRAINERS ANTI-RACIST NETWORK PO Box 28 Wallasey CH45 9NP. Tel 0151 639 1778.

INSTITUTE OF RACE RELATIONS 2 Leeke Street London WC1X 9HS. Tel 020 7833 2010.

IQRA TRUST 24 Culross Street London W1Y 3HE. Tel 020 7491 1572.

J-CORE – JEWISH COUNCIL FOR RACIAL EQUALITY 33 Seymour Place London W1H 6AT. Tel 020 8455 0896.

NALDIC – NATIONAL ASSOCIATION FOR LANGUAGE DEVELOPMENT IN THE CURRIULUM Tolpits Lane Watford WD1 8NT. Tel 01923 231855.

PLAYTRAIN 31 Farm Road Birmingham B11 1LS. Tel 0121 766 8446.

REU (formally the Race Equality Unit) 23/28 Angel Gate, City Road London EC1V 2PT. Tel 020 7278 2331.

RUNNYMEDE TRUST 133 Aldergate Street London EC1A 4JA. Tel 020 7375 1496.

STAR – SUPPORT AND TRAINING AGAINST RACISM FOR UNDER FIVES, WORKERS AND PARENTS 7 Barton Buildings Bath BA1 2JR. Tel 01225 334415.

WGARCR – WORKING GROUP AGAINST RACISM IN CHILDRENS RESOURCES 460 Wandsworth Road London SW8 3LX. Tel 020 7627 4594.

Gypsies/Travellers

ADVISORY COUNCIL FOR THE EDUCATION OF ROMANY AND OTHER TRAVELLERS Moot House The Stow Harlow CM20 3AG. Tel 01279 418666.

CAMBRIDGESHIRE and PETERBOROUGH TRAVELLER EDUCATION Foster Road Trumpington Cambridge CB2 2NL. Tel 01223 508 700.

DERBYSHIRE LIAISON GROUP Moorend Beeley, Nr Matlock, Derbyshire DE4 2NR. Tel 01629 734805.

DUBLIN TRAVELLERS EDUCATION and DEVELOPMENT GROUP Pavee Point, North Great Charles Street Dublin 1. Tel 01001 732802.

EDUCATION CENTRE FOR TRAVELLING CHILDREN Sendy Base Bradford BD4. Tel 01274 370 143.

ESSEX and SOUTHEND CONSORTIIUM TRAVELLER EDUCATION SERVICE Alec Hunter High School Stubbs Lane Braintree CM7 3NT. Tel 01376 340 360.

HARINGEY TRAVELLER SUPPORT TEAM RESOURCE CENTRE The Lodge, Church Lane London N17 8BX. Tel 020 8808 7604.

HUMBERSIDE TRAVELLER EDUCATION, Education Centre Coronation Road North Hull HU5 5RL. Tel 01482 568068.

LONDON GYPSY and TRAVELLER UNIT 6 Westgate Street London E8 3RN Tel 020 8533 2002.

NATIONAL ASSOCIATION OF TEACHERS OF TRAVELLERS c/o WMESTC The Graiseley Centre, Pool Street Wolverhampton WV2 4NE. Tel 01902 714646.

NORWICH TRAVELLER EDUCATION SERVICE Turner Road Norwich NR2 4HB. Tel 01603 766 133.

Anti-Sexism

EQUAL OPPORTUNITIES COMMISSION Overseas House Quay Street Manchester M3 3HN. Tel 0161 833 9244.

CENTRE FOR YOUNG CHILDREN'S RIGHTS (formerly Equality Learning Centre) 356 Holloway Road London N7 6PA. Tel 020 7700 8127.

Disability

ASSOCIATION FOR ALL SPEECH IMPAIRED CHILDREN 342 Central Markets London C1A 9NH. Tel 020 7236 3632.

ASSOCIATION FOR SPINA BIFIDA AND HYDROCEPHALUS 42 Park Road Peterborough PE1 2UQ. Tel 01733 555988.

BRITISH COUNCIL OF ORGANISATIONS OF DISABLED PEOPLE De Bradelei House Chapel Street Belper Derbyshire DE5 1AR. Tel 01773 828182.

BRITISH DEAF ASSOCIATION 38 Victoria Place Carlisle CA1 1HU. Tel 01228 48844.

BRITISH EPILEPSY ASSOCIATION Anstey House 40 Hanover Square Leeds LS3 1BE. Tel 0113 2439393.

COELIAC SOCIETY PO Box 220 High Wycombe Bucks HP11 2HY. Tel 01494 437278.

DYSLEXIA INSTITUTE 133 Gresham Road Staines TW18 2AJ. Tel 01784 463851.

KIDSACTIVE (formerly HAPA) Fulham Palace, Bishop's Avenue London SW6 6EA. Tel 020 7731 1435.

MENCAP – ROYAL SOCIETY FOR MENTALLY HANDICAPPED CHILDREN AND ADULTS 123 Golden Lane London EC1 0RT. Tel 020 7454 0454.

MIND Granda House 15 The Broadway London E15 4BQ. Tel 020 8519 2122.

NATIONAL ASTHMA CAMPAIGN Providence House Providence Place London N1 0NT. Tel 020 7226 2260.

NATIONAL AUTISTIC SOCIETY 276 Willesden Lane London NW2 5RB. Tel 020 8451 1114.

NATIONAL DEAF CHILDREN'S SOCIETY 15 Dufferin Street London EC1Y 8PD. Tel 020 7250 0123.

SCOPE 6 Market Road London N7 9PW. Tel 020 7619 7100.

SENSE (National Deafblind and Rube) 86 Cleveland Road London W13. Tel 020 8991 2562.

SICKLE CELL SOCIETY 54 Station Road London NW10 7UA. Tel 020 8961 7795.

UNITED KINGDOM THALASSAEMIA SOCIETY 19 Broadway London N14. Tel 020 8882 0011.

Poverty

CHILD POVERTY ACTION GROUP 1 Bath Street London EC1V 9PY. Tel 020 7253 3406.

GINGERBREAD ASSOCIATION FOR ONE PARENT FAMILIES 16 Clerkenwell Close London EC1. Tel 020 7336 8183.

OXFAM 274 Banbury Road Oxford OX2 7DZ.

SCF – SAVE THE CHILDREN 17 Grove Lane London SE5. Tel 020 7703 5400.

Other supportive organisations

BAECE – BRITISH ASSOCIATION FOR EARLY CHILDHOOD EDUCATION 136 Cavell Street London E1 2JA Tel 020 7739 7594.

CHILDREN IN SCOTLAND Princes House 5 Shandwick Place Edinburgh EH2 4RG. Tel 0131-228 8484.

DAYCARE TRUST Shoreditch Town Hall Annexe 380 Old Street London EC1V 9LT. Tel 020 7739 2866.

NCB – NATIONAL CHILDREN S BUREAU: EARLY CHILDHOOD UNIT 8 Wakley Street London EC1V 7QE. Tel 020 7843 6000.

KCN – KIDS CLUB NETWORK Bellerive House 3 Muirfield Crescent London E14 9SZ. Tel 020 7512 2112.

MINORITY RIGHTS GROUP 379 Brixton Road London SW9. Tel 020 8978 9498.

NATIONAL STEPFAMILY ASSOCIATION Chapel House 18 Hatton Place London EC1N 8JH. Tel 020 7249 2460.

NCMA – NATIONAL CHILDMINDING ASSOCIATION 8 Masons Hill Bromley BR2 9EY. Tel 020 8464 6164.

NEYN – NATIONAL EARLY YEARS NETWORK 77 Holloway Road London N7 8JZ. Tel 020 7607 9573.

NATIONAL NEWPIN Sutherland House 35 Sutherland Square London SE17 3EE. Tel 020 7701 703 6326.

PLA – PRE-SCHOOL LEARNING ALLIANCE 1 Kings Cross Road London WC1X 9LL. Tel 020 7833 0991.

REFUGEE COUNCIL 3 Bondway London SW8 1SJ. Tel 020 7820 3000.

WORKING FOR CHILDCARE 77 Holloway Road London N7 8JZ. Tel 020 7700 0281.

Bibliography

Aboud, F. and Doyle, A. (1996). Does talk of race foster prejudice or tolerance in children? *Canadian Journal of Behavioural Science*, 28(3), 161-170.

Adler, S. (1993) Aprons and Attitudes: a consideration of feminism in children's books, in H. Claire, J. Maybin, and J. Swann, (eds) *Equality Matters: Case studies from the Primary School.* Clevedon: Multilingual Matters.

Adler, S. (1993) Great Adventures and Everyday Events, in M. Barrs and S Pidgeon (eds) *Reading the Difference.* London: Centre for Language in Primary Education.

Bayley, R. (1995) A Puppet with a Problem in *Health Education No 2* MCB University Press

Berk, L. and Winsler, A (1995) *Scaffolding Children's Learning: Vygotsky and Early Childhood Education.* Washington DC, National Association for the Education of Young Children.

Bernstein, H. (1994) *The Rift.* London: Jonathon Cape.

Bisson, J. (1997) *Celebrate: an Anti-Bias Guide to Enjoying Holidays.* St Paul: Redleaf Press.

Bromley, H. (2000) Lifting the lid on the magic of storytelling in *Early Years Educator* Vol 2, No 8

Brown, B. (1994) Thinking it Over: the terminology of 'race' in *Multicultural Teaching*, Vol 12, No 2

Brown, B. (1995) Whom Do We Include: do Irish and Jewish People suffer racism? in *Nursery World* January.

Brown, B. (1998) *Unlearning Discrimination in the Early Years.* Stoke on Trent: Trentham Books.

Brown, B. (1999) *All Our Children: a guide for those who care, 4th edn*, London: Early Years Trainers Anti-Racist Network.

Brown, C., Barnfield, J. and Stone, M. (1990) *Spanner in the Works.* Stoke on Trent: Trentham Books.

Bruner, J. (1983) *Child's Talk: learning to use language.* Oxford: Oxford University Press.

Bruner, J. and Haste, H. (1987) *Making Sense: The child's construction of the world.* London: Methuen.

Cannella, G. S. (1998). *Deconstructing Early Childhood Education: Social Justice and Revolution.* New York: Peter Lang Publishing.

Cave, K. (1995) *Something Else.* London: Picture Puffins

Coard, B. (1971) *How the West Indian Child is made Subnormal in the British School System.* London: New Beacon Books.

Curriculum Guidance for the Foundation Stage (2000) London: Qualifications and Curriculum Authority

Dau, E. (1996) Exploring Families: the diversity and the issues in B. Creasner and E. Dau (eds) *The Anti-Bias Approach in Early Childhood.* Australia: Harper Educational.

David, T. Curtis, A. and Siraj-Blatchford, I. (1992) *Effective Teaching in the Early Years: fostering children's learning in nurseries and in infant classes.* Stoke on Trent: Trentham Books.

Davies, B. (1989) *Frogs and Snails and Feminist Tales: Preschool children and gender.* Sydney: Allen and Unwin.

Derman-Sparks, L. and the ABC Task Force (1989) *Anti-Bias Curriculum: tools for empowering young children.* Washington DC: National Association for the Education of Young Children

Derman-Sparks, L. (1993) *Equality in Practice.* London: Early Years Trainers Anti-Racist Network and Save the Children.

Derman-Sparks, L. and Brunson-Phillips, C. (1997) *Teaching/Learning Anti-Racism: a developmental approach.* New York: Teachers College Press.

Dixon, B (1990) *Playing Them False.* Stoke on Trent: Trentham Books.

Donaldson, M. (1978) *Children's Minds.* London: Fontana Press.

Drummond, M. J. (1997) *Reflections on Early Education and Care. Inspired by visits to Regio Emilia Italy.* London: British Association for Early Childhood Education.

Drury, R. (1997) Two Sisters at School in Gregory E. (ed.) *One Child, Many Worlds: Early learning in multicultural communities.* London: David Fulton.

Duffy, B. (1998) *Supporting Creativity and Imagination in the Early Years.* Buckingham: Open University Press.

Dunn J (1993) *Young Children's Close Relationships: beyond attachment.* London: Sage.

Edwards, V. (1995) *Speaking and Listening in Multicultural Classrooms.* Reading: The Reading and Language Information Centre.

Faber, A. and Mazlish. E. (1996) *How to Talk so Kids can Learn at Home and in School.* New York: Simon and Schuster.

Faragher, J. and Glenda MacNaughton, G. (1990) *Working with Young Children.* Collingwood, Australia: TAFE Publications.

Freire, P. 1972, *Pedagogy of the Oppressed* (Myra Bergman Ramos, Trans.). Middlesex: Penguin Books.

Gaine, B. and van Keulen, A. (1997) *Anti-Bias Training Approaches in the Early Years: a guide for trainers and teachers.* Utrecht: Agency Mutant and London: Early Years Trainers Anti-Racist Network.

Jones, K. and Mules, R. (1997) *Persona Dolls: anti-bias in action* Sydney: Lady Gowrie Child Centre

Lane, J. (1996) *From Cradle To School.* London: Commission for Racial Equality.

Lane, J. (1999) *Action for Racial Equality in the Early Years: understanding the past, thinking about the present, planning for the future.* London: The National Early Years Network

Levine, J. (1996) in *Developing Pedagogies in the Multilingual Classrom* edited by Margaret Meek. Stoke on Trent: Trentham Books.

Lynch, E and Hanson M. (eds) *Developing Cross Cultural Competence: a guide for working with young children and their families.* Paul Brooks Publishing Company: Toronto.

MacNaughton, G. (1993) A poststructuralist analysis of learning in early childhood settings. Paper presented to the Pre-Conference Symposium at the 2nd annual conference of Australian Research in Early Childhood Education, Canberra.

MacNaughton, G. (1996) The Gender Factor in B. Creasner and E. Dau (eds) *The Anti-Bias Approach in Early Childhood.* Australia: HarperEducational..

MacNaughton, G. (1997) Look! I'm Barbie and we're at Pizza Hut: the commodification of young children's identities. Paper presented to the National conference of the Creche and Kindergarten Association of Queensland, Brisbane.

MacNaughton, G.and Williams G., (1998) *Techniques for teaching Young Children: choices in theory and practice.* Australia: Addison Wesley Longman.

MacNaughton, G. (1999) Dolls for equity: young children learning respect and unlearning unfairness. Paper presented to the Persona Doll Conference, London.

MacNaughton, G. (2000) He might have to ask god! Telling silences and subtexts in how young children live with cultural diversity. Paper presented to the annual conference, Towards a Culture of Peace, Free Kindergarten Associations of Victoria.

Macpherson, W. *et.al* (1999). *The Stephen Lawrence Inquiry.* London: The Stationery Office.

Mandela, N. (1994) *Long Walk to Freedom.* Randburg: Macdonald Purnell.

McCollom, J. and Blair, H. (1994) Research in parent-child interaction:guidance to developmentally appropriate practice for young children with disabilities, in B. Mallory and R New, eds, *Diversity and Developmentally Appropriate Practices: Challenges for Early Childhood Education.* New York, Teacher's College Press.

Milner, D. (1983) *Children and Race: Ten Years On.* London: Ward Lock Educational.

Mosely, J.(1993) *Turn Your School Around.* Wisbech: Learning Development Aids.

Ogilvy C, Boath E, Cheyne W, Jahoda G and Schaffer H (1992) Staff-Child Interaction Styles in Multi-ethnic Nursery Schools, in the *British Journal of Development Psychology* Volume 10.

Oliner, S. P. and Oliner P. M. (1988) *The Altruistic Personality: rescuers of Jews in Nazi Europe.* New York: The Free Press, a division of Macmillan Inc.

Pahl, K. (1999) *Transformations: children's meaning making in nursery education.* Stoke on Trent: Trentham Books.

Paley, V. (1995) *Kwanzaa and me: a teacher's story.* Cambridge, MA: Harvard University Press.

Parekh, B. (2000) The Commission on the Future of Multi-Ethnic Britain: a summary of some of the main principles and recommendations in *Multicultural Teaching*, Vol 19, No 1.

Parkin, M. (1998) *Tales for Trainers: using stories and metaphors to facilitate learning.* London: Kogan Page.

Partington, G. and McCudden, V. (1992) *Ethnicity and Education.* Sydney: Social Science Press.

Penn, H. (2000) Hopes and Fears in *Nursery World* January 13th.

Piaget, J. (1977) *The Development of Thought. Equilibration of cognitive structures.* New York: The Viking Press.

Pogrebin, L. (1980) *Growing Up Free: Raising your child in the 80's.* New York: McGraw Hill.

Raundalen, M. (1991) *Care and Courage.* Sweden: Radda Barnen.

Richman, N. (1998). *In the Midst of the Whirlwind.* Stoke on Trent: Trentham Books.

Rieser, R. and Mason, M. (1990) *Disability Equality In The Classroom: a human rights issue.* London: Equality In Education.

Rogers, C. and Freiberg, H. J. (1994). *Freedom to Learn.* Toronto: Maxwell Macmillan Inc

Ross, C. and Browne, N. (1993) *Girls As Constructors in the Early Years.* Stoke on Trent: Trentham Books.

Saunders, K. *Happy Ever Afters: a storybook guide to teaching children about disability.* Stoke on Trent: Trentham Books.

Schiller, C, (1974) cited by Shirley Maxwell in *Preparation For Teaching in Reflections on Early Education and Care inspired by visits to Reggio Emilia, Italy.* London: British Association for Early Childhood Education.

Rutter, J. (1994) *Refugee Children in the Classroom.* Stoke on Trent: Trentham Books.

Rutter, J. (2001) *Supporting Children in 21st Century Britain.* Stoke on Trent: Trentham Books

Silin, J. (1995). *Sex, Death and the Education of Children: Our Passion for Ignorance in the Age of AIDS.* New York: Teachers College Press.

Silin, J. (1999). Speaking up for silence. *Australian Journal of Early Childhood,* 24(4), 41-45.

Siraj-Blatchford, I. (1995) Racial Equality Education: identity, curriculum and pedagogy in J Siraj-Blatchford and I Siraj-Blatchford (Eds) *Educating the Whole Child.* Buckingham: Open University Press.

Siraj-Blatchford, I. and Clarke, P. (2000) *Supporting Identity, Diversity and Language in the Early Years.*Buckingham Open University Press.

Taus, K. (1987) Teachers as storytellers for justice. Unpublished master's thesis, Pacific Oaks College, Pasadena, C.A.

Tizard, B. and Hughes, M. (1984) *Young Children Learning: talking and thinking at home and at school.* Fontana: London.

Tobin, J. (2000) *Good Guys Don't Wear Hats: children's talk about the media.* Stoke on Trent: Trentham Books.

Troyna, B. and Hatcher, R. (1992). *Racism in Children's Lives: a study of mainly white primary schools.* London: Routledge in association with the National Children's Bureau.

Volk, D. (1997). Continuities and discontinuities: teaching and learning in the home and school of a Puerto Rican five year old in Gregory E. (ed.) *One Child, Many Worlds: Early learning in multicultural communities.* London: David Fulton.

Vygotsky, L. (1978) *Mind In Society.* Cambridge Mass: Harvard University Press.

Whitehead, M. (1990) *Language and Literacy in the Early Years.* London: Chapman.

Whitney, T. (1999) *Kids Like Us: Using Persona Dolls.* St Paul: Redleaf Press.

Wood, D. and Wood, H. (1983) Questioning the Pre-school Child in *Educational Review* 35, 2 149-162.

Wright, C. (1991) *Early Years Anti-Racist Practice: Legislation and Research.* London: Early Years Trainers Anti-Racist Network.

Yates, D. *et al.* (1996) *Making it real: introducing a global dimension in the early years.* Birmingham and Coventry: Development Education

INDEX